PARAPSYCHOLOGY

BROUGHT ON

RATIONAL PEDESTAL

PARAPSYCHOLOGY

BROUGHT ON

RATIONAL PEDESTAL

NARESH KUMAR

red'shine
Publication

PARAPSYCHOLOGY BROUGHT ON RATIONAL PEDESTAL

Author: NARESH KUMAR

■

RED'SHINE PUBLICATION PVT. LTD.
Headquarters (India): 88, Patel Street, Navamuvada,
Lunawada, India-389 230
Contact: +91 76988 26988
Registration no. GJ31D0000034

In Association with,
RED'MAC INTERNATIONAL PRESS & MEDIA. INC
India | Sweden | Canada

■

■

■

ISBN: 978-93-90937-55-4 (paperback)
DIP: 18.10.554/90937
Price: ₹ 350/-
June, 2021 (First Edition)

■

■

www.redshine.co.in | info.redmac@gmail.com
Printed in India | Title ID: 90937554

To

My loving wife *Poonamji*
And my dearest children
Neema & Anshu

The book is also dedicated to
my inspirational leaders
in the field
Dr. Lance Storm
and
Dr. Sonali Marwaha Bhatt

Preface

This is my third book on Parapsychology. The first one was an introductory book and the second book was to highlight the need for trending towards Causal Research. This book is a little different as it is trying to look at Parapsychology in an unbiased rational way by including details of opponents' views and weighing the views of proponents and opponents in a rational way. My two earlier published books had a leaning towards a firm belief in paranormal events and probably had a so-called "Confirmation Bias."

Confirmation bias is the tendency to search for, interpret, favour, and recall information in a way that confirms or supports one's prior beliefs or values.

Having taken an Advanced Certificate in Parapsychology from Australian Institute for Parapsychological Research, I was passionately pursuing research in this field, and in that process, I went in pursuit of the literature which had positive views about Parapsychology without realizing that the opposing views could also be credible. This was the "***Confirmation Bias***".

I had been sifting the literature which was giving a vivid picture of astounding events manifesting in different parts of the globe - be it Telepathy, Clairvoyance, Precognition, Psychokinesis, or Life after Death. I had also gone through the history of Parapsychology and studied papers that posit interesting theories on Parapsychological phenomena. Though I had also covered the stiff opposition to the view that these phenomena are anomalous and paranormal in my work; I felt that the attack by a strong lobby of learned skeptics was because of the immense strength gained with the discovery of tricksters perpetrating frauds using magical feats or cheating tricks to prove that they possess paranormal powers displaying the parapsychological feats.

The credibility of these being really anomalous/ paranormal is dimmed with frauds surfacing up but still, it is a big question whether the Parapsychological phenomenon is anomalous/ paranormal or could it be explained by our known five senses. The "Confirmed Bias" made me look at the skeptics' views in negative light inspired only by the very few fraudulent people.
And then the realization dawned on me that my research could be improved by eliminating the tilt on one side and go in pursuit of the real truth. Ever since the realization, I started sifting through the opponents' views in the literature and now I am in a balanced state of mind so that I can do justice to the topic in a rational unbiased way and hence, I am on to this new book which treats the subject without any "***Confirmation Bias”***

I happened to read books by Caroline Watt and another by H J Irwin where they posit arguments that take a balanced view of the pros and cons of the question of Parapsychology being real or imaginary. They have posited views of researchers who try to explain the parapsychological incidents through the brain functioning or through other means which are not anomalous or paranormal. If there is an alternate explanation that has strong logic and factual basis then that would also pave a path to reach a causal conclusion quickly. Parapsychological Causal Research appears to be the final word if we do rational thinking.

This book is written to take up and discuss the subject in an unbiased manner and discuss all explanations and logic including the ones put forth by authors who claim that the incidents are not anomalous/ paranormal and can be explained by known scientific laws and the existing five senses which may be influenced by brain functions or uncommon human perceptions.

The approach is unbiased and care is taken so that author's earlier bias does not influence the logic.

The subject is being researched afresh with an open mind.
It is an interesting read…

8-5-2021 *Baroda, Gujarat, India*

Contents

Chapter 1

Why Parapsychology is still not mainstream science

In our lives we often come across events that are not perceived through our normal five senses. We have heard events where a person sitting miles away from his house perceives that there is fire around his house and it actually happened; there are occasions when someone tells you what is going in your mind and it comes to be true; some people see a relative sharing a secret known only to him and you are dumbstruck to have received the communication because the relative had died long ago; many a times premonition of an event comes true and so on.

These are baffling events and are not normal, hence, they probably, are termed Paranormal. The paranormal events are happening from time immemorial across the world.

The term "psi" is taken to notify these paranormal events. Term psi is derived from the 23rd letter of the Greek alphabet and the first letter of the word Psyche.

The study of psi forms the subject, "Parapsychology" which studies the paranormal (psi) events.

Different research organizations define psi differently but all include ESP (extra sensory Perception---which covers psi events viz., telepathy, premonition, precognition, remote viewing, clairvoyance) and PK (Psychokinesis ---influence of mind over matter viz., moving an object (without touching it) only by gazing at it) in psi definition but some even go on to include survival after death, out of body experiences, ghosts, dreams coming true and so on.. For the purpose of this book, we shall be using the term psi to indicate ESP, PK, and events of survival after death.

Psi research is going on in different parts of the world since 1882 since the formation of the Society for Psychical Research in the UK and we have come a long way from philosophical theories to Research Surveys to laboratory experimentations to meta-analysis. The big question-whether the parapsychological incidents are anomalous/paranormal is being debated and the logic and explanations in favour and against are enormous. The fact that these incidents cannot be explained by the known five senses has put enormous responsibility on researchers having their logic in favour because it is extremely difficult to put forth scientific pieces of evidence in support of their assertion. All their research efforts seem to have tilted in the direction of proving that the incidents are not mere coincidences or frauds but there is much more to it and that much more is the paranormal capabilities possessed by some humans. This tilt was necessitated due to pressure from the lobby of skeptics who, having exposed some frauds and cheating done by a handful of people, put forth their claim that the bizarre incidents coming under the purview of Parapsychology are either fraud or are figs of imagination or are the result of abnormal perception by the brain which is tricked to believe in the manifestation of the incidents.

The parapsychological research, is thus, hanging between being myth or reality, and there have appeared enormous impediments for Parapsychology being recognized as a scientific field and, still, we have not reached a stage where we can say that Parapsychology is recognized as Science. This introductory chapter studies why it is so and whether in future psi evidence can ever be accepted in mainstream science.

The apex world body on Parapsychology has the following thoughts on this issue -PA (2011):

"Parapsychology has remained controversial, even with substantial, persuasive, and scientifically palatable results, for four main reasons:

- ***First** --The media and much of the public often confuse parapsychology with sensational, unscientific beliefs and stories about "**the paranormal.**" This widespread confusion has led many scientists to simply dismiss the field as being unworthy of serious study, and thus they think it is not worth their time to examine the existing evidence. In addition, thoroughly understanding the nature of the existing evidence in parapsychology is not easy. While the meta-analytic results are both substantial and persuasive, meta-analysis requires specialized knowledge to understand that form of evidence. For people who are not familiar with statistics, or who don't trust it (which is usually a sign of misunderstanding), the evidence will not seem very persuasive. Those same people may then go looking for the big stuff, the psi-in-your-face, self-evident proofs, and they will find enormous amounts of anecdotal evidence but almost no scientifically credible data. They may then view lengthy discussions, as proof that no one really knows what is going on, and that scientists are still basically waffling and indecisive about this topic.*

  Our response is simple: The scientific evidence for some forms of psi is extremely persuasive. By the same standards used to establish proof in other areas of science, we can say with high confidence that psi does exist, and we are beginning to learn a little about it, and why people develop this gift.

- ***Second** - even if someone wanted to study the evidence, much of the persuasive work is published in limited circulation* *professional journals. In the past, these were only found in a few university libraries, with scholars needing to request reprints and technical reports from individual authors (a cumbersome process at best). Fortunately, this situation has recently changed. There is now a subscription-based online library that includes all of the journals and proceedings ever published for the Society for Psychical Research, the Journal of Parapsychology, the European Journal of Parapsychology, the Journal of Scientific Exploration, Research in Parapsychology, and Psi Researcher - Paranormal Review. It also has some books available. Best of all, the database can be searched to pull up particular words, topics, or names.*

- ***Third-*** *some people are afraid that psi might be true. For example, fear about psi arises for the following reasons:*
    1. *It is associated with diabolic forces, magic, and witchcraft.*
    2. *It suggests the loss of normal ego boundaries.*
    3. *People might be able to read your mind and know that you secretly (or unconsciously) harbor sexual and aggressive thoughts, or worse.*
    4. *If you talk about it, people might think you're crazy.*
    5. *If you think you experience psi, maybe you are crazy.*
    6. *Your parents provided negative reinforcement for any demonstrations of psychic ability (or past lives) when you were a child.*
    7. *Thinking about psi leads to a medieval superstitious mentality, which will, in turn, support a rising tide of dangerous, primitive thinking.*
    8. *With ESP, you might learn things that you do not want to know about yourself or other people -- i.e., accidents that are about to happen, and things you would rather not be responsible for knowing about.*
    9. *Psi might interfere with the normal human process of ego separation and development. Therefore, we have*

devised subtle strategies for cultural inhibition.

10. *If you are telepathic, how will you distinguish other people's thoughts from your own? Perhaps this will lead to mental illness.*
11. *Many people have a self-destructive streak to their personality. What damage would result if psi were used in the service of this factor? Psychiatrist Jule Eisenbud wrote about this in his book Parapsychology and the Unconscious.*
12. *If psi exists, how many of my other cherished beliefs will I have to give up?*
13. *If psi exists, does that mean that a psychic could watch me while I am using bathroom facilities?*
14. *If psi exists, then perhaps I cannot wall myself off so easily from the pain and suffering in the world.*
15. *With mind-matter interaction, you might have to take more responsibility for what happens--whether to you, others, or the world around you.*

(Most of the above list provided courtesy of Dr. Jeffrey Mishlove, Director of the Intuition Network)

- ***Fourth*** *as noted by Dean Radin in a talk for Google, there is a real taboo in academia about studying the paranormal. Many researchers are afraid to work or publish in the field for fear of ostracism by their colleagues. Some may even be demoted in their departments or lose their chance for tenure if they publicly speak up about their interest--even if they are only reflecting the feelings of the public majority. To put it bluntly, their reputation and careers are at stake."*

Parapsychological Association has above views to assert that there is substantial evidence to support the claim that it be accepted as a scientific field. But it is not getting rightful place in science because of unreasonable sensational publicity by media to highlight its paranormal angle, limited circulation of evidence in support, fear of getting ridiculed even if convinced about credibility, and presence of a real taboo in academia about studying the paranormal. As per Parapsychological Association, due to above four logical factors, Parapsychology is still not gaining its well-deserved place in mainstream science.

Even amongst the researching fraternity, there are divergent views taken by many parapsychological researchers—there is a strong lobby that is trying to prove that the queer incidents that are happening are not due to mere coincidences but there is much more to it and maybe some anomalous/ paranormal forces are behind the manifestation of such events. On the other hand, there are researchers who feel that the feats are tricks and frauds perpetrated by tricksters who claim to possess divine powers and they display the paranormal capabilities using fraudulent means; even employing magic tricks. And thirdly, we have renowned learned skeptics who do not believe that the Parapsychological feats are anomalous/ paranormal but can be explained by hallucinatory perception arising in the human mind (Pareidolia for instance) or are portrayed as a result of psychological deception by the claimants of psychic powers or their manifestations are just coincidences.

Parapsychological researchers, in their pursuit to bring Parapsychology under the framework of science have many impediments to tackle.

C D Broad (1949) suggests that psi tends to violate four basic principles of science, namely: -

1. *The general principle of causation - It is self-evidently impossible to have any effects before it has happened—thus precognition could not be scientific*
2. *Limitation on the action of mind on matter- An event in a person's mind can't produce directly any change in the material world except certain changes in his own brain. It is*

true that it seems to him that many of his volitions produce directly certain movements in his fingers, feet, throat, tongue, etc. These are what he wills, and he knows nothing about the changes in his brain. Nevertheless, it is these brain-changes which are the immediate consequences of his volitions; and the willed movements of his fingers, etc., follow, if they do so, only as rather remote causal descendants.

3. *Dependence of mind on the brain - Mental events which so interconnected as to be experiences of the same person are immediately conditioned by brain events that happen in the same brain. If two mental events are experiences of different persons, they are in general immediately conditioned by brain events that occur in different brains.*
4. *Limitation on ways of acquiring knowledge-- It is impossible for a person to perceive a physical event or a material thing except by means of sensations which that event or thing produces in his mind. The object perceived is not the immediate cause of the sensations by which a person perceives it. The immediate cause of these is always a certain event in the percipient's brain, and the perceived object is (or is the seat of) a rather remote causal ancestor of this brain event.*

Besides him, many other researchers, prominent among them, (Wiseman,1999; Hannah J & John Beloff, 1980; Olaf Blanke, Ortigue S &, Seeck M, 2002; Blackmore S, 1982; Wiseman R & Morris R L, 1995, Irwin H, 1985), had been explaining psi incidents in a way that brings forth different explanations to psi incidents and may support the impediments which prevent Parapsychology to enter mainstream science.

The reasons that prevent Parapsychology from being accepted as mainstream science surface up through reading vast literature are pooled and summarized here-under: -

1. Lack of commonality in the definition of subject matter --- the psi matter being discussed is not defined in a unanimous way by various parapsychological researchers/research organizations. Hannah Jenkins (University of Tasmania, Australia) considers that psi has two broad constituents- anomalous communication (ESP) and Anomalous action at distance (Psychokinesis (PK).

Whereas Parapsychological Research Organizations tend to define psi in different ways: -

Parapsychological Association (PA) considers psi to encompass telepathy, clairvoyance, remote viewing, psychokinesis, psychic healing, and precognition. Parapsychology is the study of "apparent anomalies of behaviour and experience that exist apart from currently known explanatory mechanisms that account for organism-environment and organism-organism information and influence flow" (Parapsychological Association, 1989, pp394-395).

The Venerable Society for Psychic Research of Britain takes psi to include psychical research concerning exchanges between two minds and exchanges between mind and environment which means that this encompasses a larger domain which not only includes ESP & PK but also goes on to include near death or out of body experiences, survival after death, ghosts, and hypnotic aspects. (*www.spr.ac.uk/about.html*).

American Society for Psychical Research, on the other hand, is confined to research in ESP, Psychic healing, survival after death, and dowsing. (*www.aspr.com/topics.html*)

Thus, the field of research by different researchers does not have a common core knowledge base, unlike mainstream science.

This lack of commonality approach for defining psi goes on to dilute the claim for including psi in mainstream science.

This aspect could be resolved if the different organizations come together to reach a consensus and evolve a common definition agreeable to all, hence, this is not a big obstacle. Some prominent figure in the parapsychological field has to take initiative to bring all concerned together to reach a consensus.

2. Negative definition of psi----psi happening is seen as the occurrence of an event which is not perceived through known five senses, e.g Telepathy is the transfer of information between two minds in absence of normal mechanisms which can account for it --- the definition does have a negative base.

The problem arises because psi phenomena are not defined by what they are but in terms of what they are not. Since mainstream science dwells on positive theories, psi is left behind and its study (i.e Parapsychology) does not get its place in mainstream science.

The existing five senses are not able to explain psi incidents. There could be many more senses, apart from the known five senses of perception. Could there be research to explore hitherto unknown senses and arrive at a sense and its sense organ which results in the manifestation of incidents coming under the purview of psi?

Tom Van Gelder in his paper – "Phenomenology-12 senses" suggests that are more senses in addition to the known five senses:

It was Rudolf Steiner who first proposed that there are twelve senses. His theory on senses was later expanded by various authors, including Appli, Kranich, Schoorel and Soesman.

Steiner's twelve senses can be grouped into three categories. He distinguished senses which relate to the perception of:

- your body: the senses of touch, of life, of movement, of balance
- the external world: smell, taste, sight, temperature

- the immaterial, spiritual world: hearing, speech, thought, ego

If we pursue the research on similar lines, maybe, we could discover the sense responsible for the manifestation of anomalous perception. Just imagine if we could succeed in causal research and discovered the human sense (other than the known five senses) what would happen. Irwin H J (1999) suggests – "Suppose that ESP was shown conclusively to be due to some presently recognized psychological process and was relabeled with some nameless provocative of the paranormal. In time people then might come to view such an experience no longer as incompatible with scientific principles nor as suggestive of a paranormal event, in which case the phenomenon rightly would shift from the Parapsychological domain to some other area of Psychology.

I wish that it happens and happens not only to ESP but to all psi components (including ESP) and I would love to see it happen in my lifetime and then ***having discovered this, we could redefine psi in a positive manner as is the scientific requirement.***

3. Failure to achieve replications: **-** the major factor against Parapsychology being accepted as a subject in mainstream science is that the psi events are not replicable. The psi incidents are spontaneous and sporadic and hence replication is not possible. Attempts have been made to bring psi in the laboratory and experiments have been done. JB Rhine did impressive research in the laboratory for clairvoyance where the subject was asked to guess the Zener cards (special cards developed by Zener –these had different symbols) correctly which were kept with face down. A large number of trials were done and the number of correct guesses was recorded. The correct guesses, if occurred, more frequently than the number expected by chance, psi presence was supposed to be proven. He found that many persons could do correct guessing with probability much more than the chance probability--- The statistically significant results went on to establish that psi event had happened. The laboratory experimentation by J B Rhine gained a lot of popularity and the world at large started taking telepathy seriously. The book, "Extra Sensory Perception" by J B Rhine explained psi through laboratory experimentation. His research was acclaimed by the whole world ***but it lost credibility over time by researchers when future researchers were not able to replicate results in their laboratory experimentation.***

Later Ganzfeld experiments studying telepathy in a different but improved way became popular.

In a typical ganzfeld experiment, a "receiver" is placed in a room relaxing in a comfortable chair with halved ping-pong balls over the eyes, having a red light shone on them. The receiver also wears a set of headphones through which (music called white noise or pink noise) is played. The receiver is in this state of mild sensory deprivation for half an hour. This brings the receiver in apparitions, hauntings, and a state where his psychic abilities are enhanced due to sensory deprivation. During this time, a "sender" observes a randomly chosen target and tries to mentally send this information to the receiver. The receiver speaks out loud during the 30 minutes, describing what he or she can "see". This is recorded by the experimenter (who is blind to the target) either by recording onto tape or by taking notes and is used to help the receiver during the judging procedure.

In the judging procedure, the receiver is taken out of the Ganzfeld state and given a set of possible targets, from which he selects one which most resembled the images he witnessed. Most commonly there are three decoys along with the target, giving an expected rate of 25%, by chance. A large number of experiments were conducted using the same sender and receivers and success rates were recorded. If success rate occurrence was above 25%, the telepathy success was supposed to be statistically significant and the phenomena of telepathy were thought to exist.

Palmer observed heterogeneity in the results of Ganzfeld experiments and asserted that these were not replicable.

Some researchers go on to claim that psi can never be replicated because of the psi experimenter effect. (Schmiedler & Mcconell, 1958) coined the words SHEEP (believers in psychic phenomenon) and GOAT (disbelievers in psychic phenomenon). Even varying ***Sheep-goat ability*** also is considered to affect replicability. Mainstream science does not accept theories that cannot be replicated and, hence, this is, also, one of the major factors which go against psi being accepted by mainstream science.

Alcock (2003) cites many research papers to bring home this point, rather, he goes on to say that parapsychologists have never been able to produce a demonstration that can be reliably replicated by researchers.

What we talked about above is only a subset of psi happenings- the ones we have tried to bring under experimentation categories and there can be many reasons for not attaining effective replications—poor design of experiments, experimenter's effect, sheep-goat phenomenon, environmental barriers, etc. Hence replication of results in experiments does not go against the psi phenomenon but these go against the factors which prevent the replication and it may not be possible to ensure elimination of all these factors. Moreover, in real life, the psi phenomenon is spontaneous and hence the rule of replication must not and cannot be applied as a pre-requisite for psi to come under mainstream science. ***The psi phenomenon is spontaneous, sporadic, and is happening regularly across the world, hence, instead of finding replicability, there should be causal research, results of which will pave the foundation for it to be accepted under mainstream science.***

4. Lack of continued progress in research: - Seemingly credible findings in Parapsychological Research at one time, do not get pursued in the future since new research puts question marks on the credibility of so-called credible findings. Rhine's experimental findings in card-guessing experiments (1937-1940) were considered as solid proof for the existence of psi, but the next generation found the data to be flawed and difficult to replicate, and hence future researchers totally lost interest in pursuing research further on the lines of Rhine.

A similar fate was met for remote viewing experiments by Targ and Puthoff (1974). Soal's research (Soal and Bateman 1954) which was, once, famous was later forgotten. There has been no real growth in understanding of psi, hence, further progress is not happening and we are moving in circles.

In absence of a lack of growth on the research of psi, "Parapsychology-study of psi", does not enter mainstream science. Parapsychologists must not get disheartened by results if they do not come out favourable, they must pursue causal research to reach the root cause which is making these manifest—the path is tedious and difficult and there may be frequent failures or adverse results but if we lose interest we shall never be able to bring Parapsychology being recognized as mainstream science. Causal research is the surest way in pursuit of this goal.

5. Methodological flaws in experiments: - In parapsychological research many instances are found that seemingly credible psi experiments lost credibility once a flaw was found in experimental design. Even trickery was discovered in seemingly credible phenomena.

However carefully we plan our research experiment, there remains a doubt whether we overlooked a methodological flaw. Hyman (1996) was one amongst many to point out an experimental design flaw in seemingly impeccable Ganzfeld experiments. The presence of methodological flaws is one of the factors coming in the way of the Study of psi getting accepted as mainstream science.

The discovery of experimental designs, in one way, is helping science. More and more robust designs are being developed with the accumulated learnings. The better-refined experimentations will eventually lead to scientifically justifiable research to pave the way to psi studies coming under the mainstream science.

6. Reliance on statistical methods in PSI research: - Jessica Utts (1999) is of the view that it is the role of statistics to identify and quantify important effects and relationships before any explanation is found in research. Statistical methods are of use at the discovery phase of research. Only after such a study indicates a possibility that a relationship or effect exists, the justification stage of research starts where the use of that particular field of science attempts to find causal aspects of the effect. In psi research, the statistical tool assumes a null hypothesis that the effect seen is not caused by chance only and the data collected is subjected to statistical tests of significance. In case when null hypothesis gets rejected strongly, the effect can be thought of due to some assignable cause. But finding out what those causes are is not within the scope of Statistics. The absence of chance causes does not necessarily mean that psi is the cause. Thus, even the use of statistics is not sufficient for psi to get accepted by mainstream science since causal research for psi is beyond Statistics.

It is in line with my own thinking that ultimately causal psi research will lead us to find the ultimate truth. Statistical significance will prove that assignable cause is present but that assignable cause is psi will only be established by causal psi research and we must pursue it to bring Parapsychology under mainstream science.

The aspects discussed in point nos. 4 to 6 are all for experimentation categories of psi and these barriers can at most be related to experiments and not for the actual phenomenon of psi ***which is***

spontaneous, sporadic, and is happening regularly across the world, hence, there should be causal research, results of which will remove the impediments posited in point nos. 4 to 6 and shall pave the foundation for it to be accepted under mainstream science.

7. Theorizing the event before it comes out of data: It is amusing to note Alcock (2003) referring to a quote by Sherlock Holmes, "It is a capital mistake to theorize before one has data. Insensibly one begins to twist facts to suit theories, instead of theories to suit facts." In mainstream science, we establish a theory by interpreting a lot of data. In psi research, still, the current database is not sufficient for the development of explanatory theory. Notwithstanding the absence of a good database, psi researchers, still, attempt to build theories to explain psi Phenomenon e.g., Some quantum theory models viz a quantum mechanical theory (Walker 1984) and the Thermal fluctuation model (Mattuck, 1982) proposes that the mind affects the outcome of an event by manipulating the thermal energy of molecules. Such theorizing in absence of reliable data to interpret quantum mechanical theory in such a way as to accommodate psi does not have any credibility in the eyes of a scientist, especially, a researcher in Physics. Very aptly said by Alcock (2003) "Parapsychology is motivated by a belief in search of data rather than data explaining."

This is a major flaw that pushes Parapsychology away from mainstream science. This point is valid. We still do not have enough data which could result in the evolution of a scientific theory.

The incidents are few and spread across the world, many of them are not even reported. Thus, it is a major challenge to create a needed database which when analyzed could lead to facts that take this field in mainstream science.

Whatever incidents are reported should be subjected to critical analysis with a causal approach. We must concentrate our efforts on researching the causal reasons which could be at the root of the manifestation of these events. A collective effort on part of neuroscientists, parapsychologists, psychologists, and physicists is needed to move towards causal research. In my opinion, this is the only route which will take us to reach a final conclusion whether Parapsychology can independently stand as a new branch of science or could it be explained by existing rules of science or there could evolve strong proof that each Parapsychological incident is actually a mirage and is not real but only being perceived wrongly as a hallucination. Causal research is a must and we must all move in that direction.

8. No Physical Explanation possible for PSI" -- ***John Beloff (1980)*** staunchly believes that there cannot be a physical explanation for psi. He admits that it is generally believed by some researchers that with an exploration of the unexplored portion of the mind, many unexplained events will get explained. He says that even then, psi cannot get explained because a theory which is physical cannot cover psi, and conversely a theory that encompasses psi could not be strictly physical. To make it clearer, he goes on to define what is meant by "Physical theory or explanation". He categorizes psi into ***communicational happenings or observational happenings.*** Communicational happenings are analogous to radio, radar, or telecommunication, i.e there is a transmitter and a receiver. Psi component ESP is an example of communicational happening. The observational happening of psi is those happenings in which the mind-matter relationship of psi event is observed e.g PK (Psychokinesis).

Further, he goes on to define what is ***the physical explanation or physical theory***—This is a theory that can be explained in physical terms (i.e in terms of space, time, mass, energy).

He takes up Telepathy from the communicational psi phenomenon and gives arguments why it cannot come under the category of

Physical explanation and with the same logic the finding extends to other constituents of communicational psi.

Telepathy is nothing but a transference of thoughts from one mind to another person's mind. It is difficult to surmise it in physical terms because, in this type of thought transference, the channel of using words or language does not happen because its main characteristic is that the thought transference will take place without the normal physical channels of communication e.g language. One can suggest that the thoughts could produce signals/impulses/ vibrations in the mind of the sender and these could move and get received in minds of the receptor. The question is what are the physical terms of medium which carry these and which physical means decode these vibrations in thought-form in the receptor's mind. In absence of any meaningful answer, there are no physical terms explaining Telepathy so it cannot have a physical explanation and, hence, it cannot be a physical theory or explanation.

Observational psi also cannot be explained by physical theory. He considers a PK experiment where the person's mind tries to influence the RNG machine in the generation of random numbers. Involvement of the person's mind is taken as a weak link for physical theory. The observational theorists tell that the result will depend on the state of mind i.e attitude, expectations, belief, hopes, and mood –all these will affect the outcome of results. Physical theory is not possible because we cannot specify in physical terms as to what state of mind will produce good results of PK because such state may not come in existence because the state of mind will alter for two persons or for even same person at two different times. Hence the physical theory is unlikely to explain observational psi also.

Since physical explanations are not possible for psi, mainstream science cannot accept it because it is a pre-requisite for a phenomenon to be explainable in physical terms for it to be accepted as a scientific phenomenon.

I think that psi taken to be a theory that is not physical arises out of the fact that we currently do not know the physical sense which is responsible for their perception. There has to be a physical sense in addition to the known five senses as we discussed in the above paragraphs.

Once science expands its horizons and researches to find the sense and sense organ in the human body of gifted few which is related to the perception of psi, this impediment would fade away. Till then Parapsychology will continue to be incapable of being considered as a part of mainstream science.

9. Possible trickery and other unscientific explanations of psi – Wiseman (2011) demonstrates with logic how so-called psi is nothing but trickery or a psychological way of fooling people. I will just take one example to prove his point e.g take the case of ***Fortune telling*** i.e predicting future of a person:- He believes that the so-called paranormal specialists know that people see what they want to see and they use this knowledge to frame questions/ comments keeping contradictory meaning phrases and the subject conveniently associates himself/herself with the alternative which suits him/her.

He claims that any one of us can demonstrate the ability to convince a stranger that you know all about them if you become adept in using 3 techniques, namely: - ***Flattery; Double Headed Statements and keep them vague.***

- ***Flattery***: Start by telling them what they want to hear---- look at their palm, birth date or pretend to do face reading and say that it reflects a very balanced personality, you appear to be very caring, responsible, friendly, creative, and polite and very intuitive
- ***Double-headed statements***: - Work your way through 5 key personality dimensions using double-headed sentences to describe their personality as follows: -

1. ***Open-ness***: - At times you can be imaginative and creative, but are more than capable of being practical and down to earth when necessary.
2. ***Conscientiousness***: - You value a sense of routine in some aspects of your life, but at other times, enjoy being spontaneous and unpredictable.
3. ***Extroversion***: - You can be outgoing when you want to, but sometimes enjoy nothing better than a night with a good book.
4. ***Agreeableness***: - Your friends see you as trusting and friendly, but you do have a more competitive side that emerges from time to time
5. ***Neuroticism***: - Although you feel emotionally insecure and stressed in general you are fairly relaxed and laid back

- ***Keep it Vague***: - It is fine to drop in the odd specific statement—I am getting an impression of a significant change in your life may be a journey or a change in job. I have a feeling that you are worried about a member in your family. Something gives me an impression of an important event 3 years ago in your life etc.
- Come out with abstract statements like I can see a circle closing-- does that make sense to you or I can see a door shutting –it will not open with whatever force you pull it etc. ***The subject will relate himself with the ones which are close to his /her thinking and will omit other statements from his/her memory ---this is a normal human trait. Thus, you will be taken as a knowledgeable person knowing past or future.***

Wiseman takes psi components one by one, be it Psychokinesis, Apparitions, etc. and he has explanations such as above for all these psi components which do not relate them to science.

Tricks and frauds are the most overwhelming obstacle for Parapsychology to be considered science. Human greed for fame and riches prompts people to act like fake psychics and fake mediums and claim to possess paranormal capabilities and stage performances to prove that they can manifest telepathy, clairvoyance, and psychokinesis. They use magic, hypnotism, and psychological tools to exhibit their super capabilities and when caught they not only shatter their own fate, they do irreparable damage to the credibility of Parapsychology.

All the parapsychological events are not frauds/ trickery. The fraud /trickery forms a very small part, which is restricted to staged shows or in laboratory experimentation. Widespread occurrences of paranormal incidents (across the globe) which are spontaneous and sporadic cannot be frauds/ trickery. Frauds/trickery involves planning and in spontaneous paranormal incidents planning is ruled out as there is no time to plan -these occur suddenly unannounced and hence frauds cannot be perpetrated.

Such events are real; however, their occurrence defies logic and needs causal research to really understand them.

We must consider only those incidents as constituents of Parapsychology and make efforts to find the factors which cause them –the answers will pave the way for Parapsychology to become a science in the true sense.

There is another example where the seeming psi event can have explanations other than proving it a scientific happening. I cite an example of a dream narrated on the radio (refer-transcript of radio broadcast) where the anchor ***Peter Forrest*** talks about anomalous happenings around the globe and he, then, refers to an incident narrated by Arcady Blinov who talks about a fisherman's son Mikailo Lomonosove who saw a dream that something terrible is happening to his father in midst of rough sea where he had gone fishing. Later he gets the sad news of the death of his father and he accepts the news calmly because he had seen all this in a dream. The son astonishes the messenger when he goes on to describe finer details of the incident of his father meeting death at rough sea-- which could be possible only if he was personally present there.

Discussions happen to analyze why such a dream was seen by the son.

The logical reasoning given is that the mind can store infinite situations as perceived or heard in past and can reconstruct them in a logical sequence to connect them in the dream when we go to sleep with anxiety on the topic. Various possibilities are there, in past the fisherman could have taken son on fishing expeditions and told him about the dangers that lay in fishing in the rough sea, his mother could have forewarned about the dangers in the sea and all those got registered in the subconscious and finally culminated in the dream which encompassed fine details as to how his father could meet a tragic end. It is possible that similar dream could have come many times earlier also but did not register importance. Only on this occasion since death actually happened it looked like a psi happening. Wiseman (1999) also touches on this point in the way as explained above as he goes on to say that daily we see dreams but we forget them as nothing relating to dream comes near to actually happening but the day we have some incident faintly resembling the dream, it becomes a memorable event.

Coincidence is one aspect that holds ground against Parapsychology and is a formidable obstacle in the way of Parapsychology being taken in the lap of mainstream science. Coincidence means that the event happened by chance. This aspect is taken seriously by Parapsychologists and they resorted to laboratory experiments where they have conducted experiments to test the hypothesis that telepathy (Ganzfeld experiments) and Clairvoyance (card-guessing experiments) occur due to chance. The statistical analysis proves beyond doubt in many experiments that the event happened not by chance cause but by assignable cause. The statistical evidence before us is indicative that the manifestation of the events is not mere coincidence but the incidents may be really anomalous.

Skeptics have tried to refute these proofs by suggesting flaws in experimental designs and the inability of repeatability. However carefully we design an experiment, there remains a possibility of some flaw in the design. Also, replication is not happening due to the absence of several unknown factors which may be missing in the attempts of replication, exact design replication being one of the factors.

Whether the spontaneous parapsychological events occur only by mere chance is difficult to say. Irwin H J (1999) posits the same view: "Perhaps the major argument against the use of spontaneous case material for the purpose of authenticating parapsychological phenomena is that the role of chance in such cases is unknown. You may intuit the unlikelihood of a given case being due purely to coincidence but the fact remains that almost invariably the investigator is not able to specify the statistical probability of the event's occurrence by chance."

Even though in experimental research, there is overwhelming statistical evidence that the results go on to prove that the probability of occurrence is more than that of chance but for spontaneous parapsychological incidents, as of now, this impediment is beyond resolution.

The point made in the above narration not only points out that psi cannot relate itself to mainstream science but goes on to bring MIND's interference to explain how the mind's working can make an event look like a psi event when in fact it is not. This is an important aspect that I would like to connect to when I am concluding this chapter with a futuristic view of psi and mainstream science.

The above obstacles and also Broad's views on psi violating basic principles of science together go on to build a strong case that Parapsychology cannot become a part of mainstream science.

The way forward

We have observed that psi incidents are unexplainable by scientifically known five senses of perception. However, it is also a fact that the incidents do happen and we are not able to deny their physical occurrence. It is true that we are unable to find causative reasoning because the self-imposed definitions have limited scientific scope to explain the happenings in physical terms.

In the above discussion on the dream ----the mind is stipulated to work in a way to create a dream which is very-very near to the incident that really happened. Mind played a pivotal role to construct the dream and make it look as if a psi event has happened. It is a fact that ESP / PK brings mind as a factor because mind to mind or mind to matter is the base to the parapsychological phenomenon.

A causal explanation is currently not possible because most of the capabilities of the mind are still hidden and beyond our reach. Mind is still a far cry; we do not even know about most part of the brain.

Parapsychologists, Psychologists, Medical researchers, Physicists, and Neuroscience researchers must collaborate together to pursue mind-brain research so that they uncover the mystery surrounding causal roots behind psi and this would be the first step towards bringing psi into mainstream science. I tend to agree with the above and my logic is simple---psi currently does not come under the helm of mainstream science because, by definition, the psi happenings are not physically explainable by the known five senses and we are yet to discover through the above research the hitherto unknown sense and the sense organ which result in the manifestation of psi incidents-Brain is still not fully explored, maybe there exists a psi sense which is still not explored. Neuroscience researchers while researching the brain may come out with a nerve circuitry system in the brain consisting of, hitherto unknown, arrangement of neurons and synapses (Michael O' Shea, 2005) which can sniff and make psi happenings explainable through a sixth sense, a psi sense, which presently is a proverbial sixth sense. If that happens, then we shall not have to take recourse to the negative way of defining psi and it will be defined in a positive way as it will be linked to the researched sixth sense. Then psi will have a positive and deterministic physical explanation which will be, probably, the first step to pave way for it to be recognized by mainstream science and philosophy.

The causal reason for Consciousness is, also, not fully understood yet. Further advances in research on "consciousness" will throw open answers to hitherto unknown channels by which the paranormal is getting perceived and only a collaborative effort as suggested above will lead us to explain Consciousness, the psi sense, and the psi organ.

The mystery will unfold with advancement research concerning brain, mind, and consciousness and the advancement in research will prove as a boon to parapsychological research---- but that is the future and the future is unpredictable.

Till then we keep our fingers crossed for finding the answer to the question raised in this chapter.

Next, we move on to take on individual constituents of Parapsychology and try to put them on a rational pedestal by discussing the proponent and opponent views and trying to find a midway acceptable to both.
We start with Telepathy.

Chapter 2

Telepathy- on a rational pedestal

One morning, while a young boy, Hans was on horseback during a training exercise, his horse suddenly reared. Hans was tossed into the air and he landed hard on the road, directly in the path of a fast approaching, horse-drawn cannon. He realized with horror that he was about to be crushed, but the driver of the cannon managed to stop the horses in time. The accident left Hans thoroughly shaken but without serious injury. At the same very moment, many miles away in his family's home, his older sister was suddenly overwhelmed with an ominous certainty that something bad had happened to Hans. She anxiously insisted that her father sent him a telegram. .... Hans on receiving the telegram knew that his feelings of intense fear had somehow reached his sister. Many years later, Hans wrote, "This is a case of spontaneous telepathy in which at a time of mortal danger, I transmitted my thoughts and my sister, who was particularly close to me, acted as the receiver"

(an incident in the life of Mr. Hans Berger who gave the world "EEG": Dean Radin (2006)-Entangled Minds)

If we look at the history of telepathy, incidents as above had been reported from time immemorial.

"Telepathy" is derived from the Greek terms tele (*"distant" or "distance"*) and pathe (*"occurrence" or "feeling"*). So, Telepathy actually means getting feelings through a distance.

The term was coined in 1882 by the psychical researcher ***Fredric W. H. Myers***, one of the founders of the Society for Psychical Research (*SPR*).

Myers thought his term described the phenomenon better than previously used terms such as the French *"communication de pensees,"* "thought-transference," and *"thought-reading."*

To elaborate, Telepathy is the communication between two minds, separated over a distance, without the use of the five known senses.

At some point or the other, we all have experienced Telepathy. Maybe you were thinking of someone you haven't talked to in months and you suddenly get a call from him. Or when two people are together, they might say the same thing at the same time. These are spontaneous ***mind-to-mind communication***. *psy-minds.com/telepathy-mental-communication*)

Rightly said in the above paragraph, Telepathy is commonly understood as the mind-to-mind connection. The connection is direct without the involvement of our known five senses.

One common experience which we all may have had is that we, unconsciously, reflexively, do yawning when we see someone yawn. Why do we do that? Is this mind-to-mind connection that compels us to do it?

I felt that I found the answer while reading a book by V S Ramachandran (2012) wherein he talks about 'Mirror Neurons' – he talks about a neurosurgeon who finds a neuron becoming active when he poked the patient with a needle. He was further astonished when the same patient watches another patient who is poked with a needle and the same neuron again becomes active i.e., the neuron senses pain even when the patient himself is untouched but he is only watching another patient in pain. Such neurons are known as "Mirror neurons". The mirror neurons helped to connect two minds of two people and the sense of pain was felt through mind-to-mind connection i.e., without the use of normal five senses--- but that is exactly what telepathy is!

Knowledge of 'mirror neurons' came as a delightful knowledge to me and I realized that the reflex yawning action on seeing someone yawn must be due to these mirror neurons at work.; which means that they are responsible for Telepathy---Mirror neurons are then the scientific basis for Telepathy--- Eureka!!

Maybe then telepathy is not the mind-to-mind connection but is the brain-to-brain connection. In a delightful mood, I got in touch with my inspirational leader in the psychological field, Dr. Lance Storm of the Australian Institute of Parapsychological Research, and shared with him my delightful finding and put a question to him whether Telepathy could be due to 'Mirror Neurons'. His answer brought me back to cold reality!

He said it was not so; he elaborated his answer by explaining to me that telepathy at short distances when people can see each other, is being explained by you by 'mirror neurons", but telepathy works even at long distances-how do you explain them? True- the Hans incident above could not be due to mirror neurons!

My delight was short-lived and I understood that the subject is not easy and needs further deep research. The common experiences even at far distances have got to be researched to understand Telepathy.

Turning to another common experience we all may have gone through some time or the other is that even with closed eyes, we get a feeling of uneasy sensation that somebody is staring at us and we find that we are being stared at. This is more common with women, who, even without looking, become conscious that they are getting stared at by some men and they find that in fact, someone was, actually, staring at them.

Why does this happen? Why are we able to feel uneasiness with a simple stare by some other person? Is it that the act of staring is a result of a focused impact from the mind of the person who is staring to the mind of stared; is it that the mind of a person (who is staring) is releasing some energy which is received by the mind of stared; resulting in uneasiness and discomfort in him/her? Does focused attention compel the mind to accumulate this energy and release it to result in the form of uneasiness?

Could it be Telepathy at work in closed proximity-mirror Neurons?? What is this energy? Is it animal magnetism at work (without touch) as was propagated by Mesmer?

While writing the above lines, I was thinking that these are my original thoughts based on my observational instinct but, later, I got a pleasant surprise when I came across literature which talks about the staring event:

Sheldrake Rupert (1998) talks about simple experiments that were carried out in schools in Germany and the United States to test whether or not people can tell when they are being stared at from behind. Lookers and subjects worked in pairs, with the lookers sitting behind the subjects. In a series of trials, the lookers either looked or did not look at the subjects in a random sequence determined by tossing a coin. In each trial, the subjects guessed whether or not they were being looked at. The results show an overall positive effect, with 56.9% correct guesses as opposed to 50% expected by chance. In one school in Germany where sensitive subjects were tested repeatedly, 71.2% of the guesses were correct, and two students were right about 90% of the time.

So, it is observed by others as well that unseen staring does impact the stared. It could be mind-to-mind communication i.e., Telepathy. (Naresh Kumar, 2021)

The telepathic incidents of varying nature are so common that each of us in our life has some time or the other have exclaimed, "How could this happen?" Maybe there are occasions when you remember a friend staying abroad and at that moment you get a what's app call and when you respond you find that friend on the line. There are occasions when you feel uneasy and later you learn that some of your loved ones were being taken to hospital precisely at that time.

The incidents like above are commonly observed incidents that happen in our lives and momentarily we are surprised and soon after we forget them as mere coincidences and do not attach much importance to it nor consider these as worthy for deeper probing and study. The literature is full of incidents ranging from routine incidents to mind baffling and unbelievable.

Look at the following Telepathic incident:
Joshua Hehe narrates a Telepathic incident: "In 1955 a Wisconsin housewife named Joicey Hurth was washing dishes when suddenly she became certain that her daughter was about to be killed. She later learned that at the time she received the impression that her daughter was in danger, the girl had been hit by a car and seriously injured, though not killed. Hurth's experience is an example of one of the most common incidents of telepathy, in that it occurred when the apparent sender of the telepathic message was in crisis.

Moreover, according to one study by Ian Stevenson, a professor of psychiatry at the University of Virginia, nearly 70 percent of telepathic incidents involve close family members, whereas approximately 28 percent of such incidents occur between friends or acquaintances and only 2 percent between strangers."

It is generally observed that telepathic incidents occur more when there is some emotional turmoil in the life of the sender of the message and mostly telepathy happens between close relations even at long distances.

Commonly it is thought that the person in emotional turmoil is the sender of a telepathic message and the receiver is just a passive entity receiving the telepathic message. Louisa Rhine has something different to say in this regard: "*Louisa Rhine speculated that in ESP the notion of an agent sending a message to the experient might be invalid. Rather, the experient may be the "active" member of the association, in some way seeking out information on people emotionally close to him or her. Support for this idea emerged in a later study (Rhine 1956) in which it was found that although experients in telepathic cases did need to know about the agent, in about a sixth of the cases there seemed to be no conceivable reason for the agent to communicate to the experient. Louisa Rhine's suggestion certainly raises questions about the popular view of extrasensory "perception" as a perceptual-like process or a "sixth sense" in which some unidentified sort of environmental "stimulus" is mediated to a percipient.*

The most interesting idea thrown up by Louisa Rhine's analyses of spontaneous case reports is that ESP seems purposive in its orientation and that it may well be instigated by the experient rather than being received passively by him or her." (Irwing H J (1999)

Whether the telepathic message is sent by the sender or the receiver being the "active" agent somehow gets the message; the basic fact is that mind to mind connection does get established and in most cases, the emotional turmoil is there in the manifestation of telepathic incidents overcoming distance barriers, leaving aside exceptional cases of telepathy in proximity like yawning and staring which were discussed earlier.

How does telepathy manifest defying known senses and overcoming distance barriers? Is the phenomenon scientific and real, or is it anomalous or paranormal? *It is difficult to find an answer.*

Through telepathic and clairvoyant means, the Psychics have claimed to be able to offer personal advice, solve crimes, locate missing people, and help gather intelligence for government agencies. Researching these claims is often problematic because the work has to take place outside the confines of a controlled laboratory environment. (Caroline Watt, 2016).

There have been experimental attempts (through Ganzfeld Experiments) to investigate telepathy. Caroline Watt (2016) gives an account of that: *"Parapsychologists have developed different methods for researching the possible existence of telepathy and clairvoyance. In Rhine's early work, this involved participants attempting to guess the identity of Zener cards. At Maimonides Dream Laboratory researchers explored whether the dream state was associated with psychic functioning. Finally, in Ganzfeld procedure, participants are placed in a situation where sensory distractions are minimized and are asked to describe a remote target (thought by the sender of the telepathic message). The researchers carrying out these studies have claimed the results of the work support the existence of ESP. Some of these claims have been published in leading mainstream psychological journals, indicating that the work is judged to have met high scientific standards. Despite this, some skeptics have argued that these studies contain methodological and statistical shortcomings. Although not all of this criticism has been deserved, overall the field has benefitted from such scrutiny because it has led to a range of methodological improvements, including those designed to minimize publication bias, sensory leakage, and poor randomization. Indeed, such improvements may be one of the greatest benefits to come out of the work. Robert Rosenthal stated, "Science in general and parapsychological inquiry, in particular, have been well served by the recent ganzfeld debate."*

Caroline Watt does not assert that telepathy can be termed a scientific phenomenon but she points out that the research work claiming that Telepathy exists has been accepted by world fame psychology journals which means that it has a nod of the scientific community. On the other hand, she is also not supportive to the claims of skeptics who point that the shortcomings in experimental design could have led to sensory leakages and, thus, create doubts on the existence of telepathy.

But Caroline Watt does admit that the proof provided by the Ganzfeld experiments about the existence of Telepathy is overwhelming and cannot be brushed aside and goes on to admit that refinement of parapsychological experimental research has made a significant contribution to Parapsychology and science through achieving a range of methodological improvements, including those designed to minimize publication bias, sensory leakage, and poor randomization in the experimental designs.

We do not know whether Telepathy can still get considered a scientific phenomenon but it is a fact that telepathic incidents do happen and it is a reality.

Telepathy is generally considered a special ability that rare people possess across the world but it is said that in tribal societies such as the ***Aborigines of Australia***, telepathy is accepted as a human faculty.

Elkin (1930) collected many reports of psychic phenomena, later published in a book in 1944. Ordinary Aborigines had psychic powers only at times, such as on the death of a relative. Their psychic abilities resulted from openness to experience, lack of attention to time, and the quiet and solitude of the bush. Anecdotes included seeing spirits, healing (in part, psychic surgery), sorcery, ***telepathy over huge distances***, X-ray vision, sending the "dream familiar" out of the body, hypnotism, and fire walking. (*https://www.aipriinc.org/aboriginal/*)

If it is a fact that Telepathy is commonly found in some tribes, the question of whether it is scientific would amount to find the scientific basis of this faculty being frequent in the tribe and what is common between the tribes and rare people scattered across the world who possess this special ability. We shall need to understand what is distinct in the tribe from the world at large.

On similar lines of a tribe possessing this faculty, it was observed that such faculty also existed in people influenced by mesmerism. In fact, research interest in telepathy had its beginning in Mesmerism. It is said that Mesmer (1733-1815 while experimenting on the effect of magnets in physiological functions of the body (e.g., blood flow rates) realized that there existed energy in the universe which flows in our body as well, and if the distribution of this energy is balanced, the body remains healthy. Imbalance leads to sickness and health disorders.

He termed this energy in the body as "Animal Magnetism". To treat health disorders; animal magnetism could be transferred from a healthy body to the patient to bring uniformity of this energy to cure the person. The transference could be done simply by touch. He could cure many patients having fits and seizures. He and his disciples, while doing this therapy, found that their patients, during therapy went to a sleep-like state and were responding to their commands. The phenomenon became popular as, "Mesmerism", which ultimately, over a period of time developed to "Hypnotism"- a therapy used even now by Psychologists to treat patients with mental disorders. Not only that but, the use of a trance-like mental state is also made in current experimental parapsychological research.

Some of Mesmer's patients, in a sleep-like state, were able to gain access to information/events that were inaccessible to them through normal means, e.g., describing actions done by a person in another room. These were first-ever known instances of Telepathy witnessed under controlled conditions. The magnetics discovered that telepathy was among the so-called "higher-phenomena" observed in magnetized subjects, who read the thoughts of the magnetics and carried out the unspoken instructions.

Other psychologists and psychiatrists were observing the same phenomena in their patients. Sigmund Freud noticed it so often that he had to address it. He termed it a regressive, primitive faculty that was lost in the course of evolution, but which still had the ability to manifest itself under certain conditions. Psychiatrist Carl G. Jung thought it more important. He considered it a function of synchronicity. (*positivemed.com/2014/03/10/telepathy-real/*)

Synchronicity is a phenomenon in which people interpret two separates—and seemingly unrelated—experiences as being meaningfully intertwined, even though there is no evidence that one led to the other or that the two events are linked in any other causal way. Though many people perceive signs or spiritual meaning in synchronistic events, most scientists believe that such events are more likely coincidences that only seem meaningful due to aspects of human thinking such as confirmation bias. The concept of

synchronicity was developed by psychiatrist and psychoanalyst Carl Jung in the early 1900s. Jung himself believed in synchronicity, which he defined as "meaningful coincidences." (*www.psychologytoday.com/us/basics/synchronicity*)

In simpler words, telepathy, as per Carl Jung is nothing but a meaningful coincidence and nothing beyond that. Events happening by chance could not qualify for being a scientific phenomenon. However, it will be incorrect to agree with Carl Jung's thoughts because his theory is thrashed out by subsequent laboratory experiments on Telepathy which yielded statistically significant results to prove that the experimental results were not happening by chance and had some assignable causes responsible for them. The results were credible and were accepted by scientific journals as observed by Caroline Watt as was discussed in earlier paragraphs. Meta-analysis of telepathic experiments is also suggestive that probability for the positive results is statistically significant above chance level.

However, not that these results were accepted by all, there have been influential skeptics who claim that statistically significant results indicating that the probability of their occurrence is above chance levels could be due to some flaw in experimental design. Even the experiments done in extremely controlled conditions leave a doubt in minds of skeptics that there could be a flaw in the design of the experiment. Moreover, probabilistic findings need to be confirmed by further causal research to establish the causal aspects of the phenomenon with certainty—this is still to happen.

While causal telepathic research is yet to see the light of the day, which will clear all doubts but currently it is observed that Telepathy seems to be related to the individual's emotional state. This is true of both the sender and receiver.

Geriatric telepathy is fairly common, this may be due, it is speculated, to the impairment of the senses with age. Telepathy can be induced in the dream state. It appears to be related to some biological factors: blood volume changes during telepathic sending and electroencephalogram monitoring show that the brain waves of the recipient change to match those of the sender. Likewise – dissociative drugs adversely affect telepathy, but caffeine has a positive effect on it.

During his 1930 ESP experiments, J. B. Rhine also made some discoveries concerning telepathy: It was often difficult to determine whether the information was communicated through telepathy, clairvoyance, or precognitive clairvoyance. He concluded that telepathy and clairvoyance were the same psychic function manifested in different ways. Also, telepathy is not affected by distance or obstacles between the sender and receiver. (*positivemed.com/2014/03/10/telepathy-real/*)

The evidence so far suggests that the telepathic incidents are real and experimental results also show that they do not happen by chance. However, skeptics say that the positive results could have happened due to sensory leakage owing to a fault in the design of experiments. Also, there is another lobby of tricksters whose actions result in dimming the credibility of Telepathy. Rhine (1938, p. 151) has stated: "The goal of the experimenter is the complete exclusion of all possible sensory cues, which includes assuming the dishonesty of the subject," and "if under the conditions deception is humanly possible, the conditions are not adequate to establish the degree of confidence required for so weighty a conclusion as the occurrence of extra-sensory perception." Although many people subscribe to this approach, it is not universally shared. Some believe that the burden is on the skeptic to prove cheating occurred in an experiment rather than it is the responsibility of the experimenter to safeguard against trickery. Parapsychological Association presidential message said that "fraud detection and prevention is a rich, complex area of endeavour in itself; yet it is also very appropriately a part of the domain of parapsychology"

However, frauds and tricks do happen and reduce the credibility of Telepathy. Hansen George P (1990) has the following views regarding frauds/tricks in Telepathic experiments: "*Telepathy experiments involve special considerations with regard to subject trickery. In fact, this difficulty has been long recognized. Rhine and Pratt (1957/ 1962) state: With GESP and pure telepathy, precautions have to be elaborate and have to be adapted to the special needs of the experimental situation. This methodological problem is often taken too lightly; as we have said, GESP is the hardest psi-test procedure to control adequately against error, especially error due to deception.*

There have been a number of historical instances that have shown this to be a serious problem. The early SPR investigated the team of G. A. Smith and Douglas Blackburn and found evidence for telepathy (Gumey, Myers, Podmore, & Barren, 1883). Later Blackburn issued a confession as to how they had deceived the researchers, but Smith denied it (see "Confessions of a 'Telepathist'," 1911; Coover, 1917, pp. 477–495; Gauld, 1965a, 1965b, 1968, pp. 179–182; Hall, 1964, 1968; Nicol, 1966; and Oppenheim, 1985, pp. 285–286 for extended coverage of the affair). Whatever be the ultimate truth of the matter, the experimental precautions did not rule out the possibility of collusion between agent and percipient. Barrett, Gumey, and Myers (1882) also investigated the alleged telepathic abilities of the Creery sisters. Here, too, precautions were not always sufficient to rule out collusion, and later the sisters confessed to cheating (Gumey, 1888; for discussion see Coover, 1917, pp. 463–477; Hall, 1964; "Psychological Literature," 1887). Soal and Bowden (1960) conducted numerous telepathy studies with several Welsh children; during a few of the experiments, two boys were detected using codes to signal each other. This led to some discussion as to how much cheating was actually involved (e.g., Mundle, 1959; B. H. Nicol, 1960; J. F. Nicol, 1960; Scott & Goldney, 1960; Soal, 1959, 1960; Thouless, 1961).

The most severe problem faced by experimenters is the possibility of the sender signaling the receiver. There are innumerable ways of doing this, and a huge number of methods have been incorporated into commercially available magic tricks. Dingwall (1956) has given a very brief historical overview of simulations of telepathy.

Some suggested methods for use in psi experiments include high-pitched whistles (Hansel, 1959; Scott & Goldney, 1960), subtle changes in lighting conditions (Estabrooks, 1947, pp. 122–126), radio transmitters (Soal & Bowden, 1960), and even transmitters hidden in teeth (Targ & Puthoff, 1974).

Morris (1978) has pointed out that a signaling method might be implemented in forced-choice situations in which the sender signals the receiver for the next trial. One could send a slightly longer or shorter signal depending upon the target. An alternative method is to send the signal at certain times. Annemann (1938) suggested that the interval between signals could be used as a code. On the other hand, in typical psi experiments, it is acceptable for the receiver to signal the sender when ready for the next trial, as noted by Rhine and Pratt (1957/1962).”

Hansen's peep into possible ways of frauds in telepathic experiments is very vivid and such instances certainly taint the credibility of the telepathic phenomenon.

Even the telepathic incidents happening outside the laboratory are considered as mere meaningful coincidences-Synchronicity.

In conclusion, we can say that the above impediments prevent telepathy to be considered as a science, whereas on the other hand, the telepathic incidents are real and not figs of imagination. In my opinion, even though, there is substantial evidence that shows that the positive results in experiments are not achieved through chance or coincidence but for incidents outside the laboratory, it is difficult to make a similar statement. The spontaneous sporadic telepathic incidents happen but still why these happen is not known and simply dismissing them as coincidence is not appropriate because of an enormous number of such events being reported from across the globe.

The doubts will be cleared only through casual telepathic research which will establish the root cause behind the manifestation of telepathy and then only the telepathic perception would have answered the question conclusively whether Telepathy Phenomena is scientific in affirmative or otherwise!!

I have not come across much literature on causal research on telepathy. Causal research is the only way to reach an answer to the question of whether telepathy could be science or not and we must take the first step towards causal telepathic research. I did suggest some subtle ways to initiate this research in my book-*Parapsychology-trending towards Causal Research,* I shall be dwelling on the ways how causal telepathic research can be initiated using my thoughts presented in the book.

Trending towards Causal Telepathic Research

At the onset, I wish to make it clear that I am not an authority to criticize research done hitherto nor is my intention of doing so. Work done so far is valuable beyond doubt and has brought credibility to Parapsychology. I am still in the process of digging into the vast literature and daily I am adding to my knowledge. Eminent scientists and researchers including my inspirational scholars in the field are busy researching and newer ideas and newer theories are emerging. I, only, humbly suggest whether we can start thinking about causal reasoning also, which could explain paranormal events.

Therefore, my humble submission is that we must devote some of our efforts (a beginning appears to have been done by Dr. Sonali and Prof. May and Dean Radin) towards Causal Parapsychological research. Maybe the approaches as outlined in the coming paragraphs will help; there can be many more, which could emerge through the innovative thinking of researchers.

Coming to the field of Telepathy- we know that telepathy is mind to mind connection- it is thought transference between two minds unlimited by distance. To start causal reasoning, we have to first think about how could we do thought transference in a controlled way and then extend our research to probe further. Can we externally capture thoughts going in our minds?

The question was weighing in the mind of a genius Nichola Tesla during the last days of his life. Nikola Tesla, the genius working on electrical energy during Edison's time. He was toying with an idea that thoughts in mind reflect, by reflex action, a picture on our retina and it could be possible to capture the same on an external apparatus. When he died, he was working on a project involving "Thought Projector"

Smith (2017) in his paper, ***"Nikola Tesla's wildest Project-Thought Projector",*** mentions "When Nikola Tesla died, he left behind fascinating writings about inventions he never realized. One such invention is ***DER GEDANKENPROJEKTOR,*** a camera that could be used to photograph thoughts.

Tesla (1933) argued that if it is true that thought reflects an image on the retina, it is merely a question of illuminating the same properly and taking photographs & then using ordinary methods which are available to project an image on the screen.

"If this could be done then the objects imagined by a person would be clearly reflected on the screen as and when they are formed, and, in this way, each thought of the individual could be read. Our minds would then be "***Open books***"

Tesla's line of research is an extension of the fact that things don't need to be seen only with open eyes, one could, even, see things with closed eyes; the only difference is that the objects perceived are not external but within the self --- i.e., images, instead of coming from the open eye, these can come directly to the retina as reflex images from thoughts created by the mind and the rest of perception activities in the brain continues as they do normally.

Tesla's thinking seems to be credible; thoughts, by reflex actions, must be producing images on the retina, how else could we see dreams??

In fact, dreams may be thoughts portrayed as motion pictures that get reflected on the retina and through the normal processes of these getting converted into electrical impulses passing on information to neurons and synapses to make us see them as movies while asleep.

Bahar Gholipour (2014) mentions, "Tesla's plans never became a reality but researchers are still studying ***vision*** and exploring the idea of building mind-reading machines.

With machines becoming capable of reading minds, we may get a clue from their work and could then understand how the mind does read mind and how telepathy manifests. Maybe, then we would be possible to take a cue and develop a capability in us to directly see the thought pictures and thereby learn the thoughts going on in other's mind.

If our scientists could invent such innovative equipment, we would have opened a door that offers a clue to get at bottom of the mystery of ***"Telepathy".***

Physicists, neuroscientists, and medical researchers may, one day, come up with a solution to telepathy following Tesla's footsteps.

There is another scientific development worth mentioning here which could lead to another approach towards causal research on Telepathy.

Ralph Lewis (2019) illustrates what thoughts are and how the information is physical?

As per him, "Fundamentally, our thoughts are maps which represent and correspond to things that our brains have either perceived with our senses, felt with our emotions, or formed as an action plan. All of these are electrochemically mediated processes. Thoughts may be fleeting, or they may later be consolidated as memories. Memory too is a physical process, encoded by structural molecular changes in neuronal connections.

Sensory perceptions and their memories are physical representations or maps, imprinted by an event"

He goes on to suggest the possibility of Telepathy as follows, "Since thoughts are physical and have spatial dimensions (each thought being represented by complex connections between large arrays of neurons), you might wonder if it's possible to 'read' a person's thoughts from their brain's patterns of neuronal activity. In fact, scientists have already been on that project for several years.

Today Scientists have created ***artificial retinas*** through sophisticated mathematical analyses of how real retinas convert images to electrical impulses to send to the brain. In attempts at mind-reading, scientists have developed algorithms that can learn to interpret brain signals and reproduce a rough version of images "seen" in a person's mind"

On thoughts, Taylor (1998) says "The theory proposes that the contacts may be due to interactions between fields corresponding to the appraisals of thoughts about events. It is suggested that when thoughts are appraised, a field is created which gives rise to the subjective feeling of emotion. If at a later moment, the same thoughts are repeated and they are similarly appraised, then another field will be created which has a similar structure to the first one. The fields interact and 'resonate' together. This not only increases the degree of emotion associated with the thoughts but also enables precognition to occur by increasing the attention drawn to the earlier thoughts. Telepathy similarly occurs when the thought appraisals correspond to those of another person. The mechanism allows precognition to occur without raising the intervention paradox."

There is one more interesting paper that can open doors to understanding the mystery behind Telepathy:

Matthews Hutson (2018), in his paper, "*Mind-reading algorithm can decode the pictures in your head*" suggests that, "Now scientists have created the first algorithm of its kind to interpret- and accurately reproduce—images seen or imagined by another person. It might be decades before the technology is ready for practical use, but researchers are one step closer to building systems that could help us project our inner mind's eye outward... Using algorithms to decode mental images is not new. Since 2011, researchers have created movie clips, photos, and even dream imagery by matching brain activity to activity recorded earlier when viewing images. But these methods have all their limits: some deal with only narrow domains like face shapes, and others can't build an image from scratch— instead they must select from pre-programmed images or categories like "person" or "bird". This new work can generate recognizable images on the fly and even reproduce the shapes that are not seen, but imagined.

He is hopeful that with better measurements in algorithms, we might someday communicate thru mental pictures."

Another paper throws open avenues for causal research on Telepathy. The advancement in brain imaging has posited new facts as brought out in a paper by Venkatasubramanian Ganesan, Jayakumar Peruvumba, Nagendra Hongasandra, Nagaraja Dindagur, Deeptha R, Gangadhar Bangalore (2008), point out that we have located a portion in the brain where the processing of Telepathy may be taking place. In their paper they highlight this point:

"Telepathy" is defined as "the communication of impressions of any kind from one mind to another, independently of the recognized channels of sense". Meta-analyses of "Ganzfeld" studies as well as "card-guessing task" studies provide compelling evidence for the existence of telepathic phenomena. This study aimed to elucidate the neural basis of telepathy by examining an individual with this special ability. Materials and Methods: Using functional MRI, we examined a famous "mentalist" while he was performing a telepathic task in a 1.5 T scanner. A matched control subject without this special ability was also examined under similar conditions. Results: The mentalist demonstrated significant activation of the right parahippocampal gyrus after the successful performance of a telepathic task. The comparison subject, who did not show any telepathic ability, demonstrated significant activation of the left inferior frontal gyrus. Conclusions: The findings of this study are suggestive of a limbic basis for telepathy and warrant further systematic research."

A similar observation is found for connecting Telepathy with the ***Parahippocampal region of the brain***, in a separate study of brain patterns in a person, Sean Harribance, undergoing telepathic feat are brought out by Michael Persinger and Kevin S Saroka (2012)-

"The raw data from the unique EEG pattern displayed by Sean Harribance during his intuitive state revealed a peak increase of power within the upper beta region (20- 30 Hz) within the Parahippocampal region only.

The congruence of the region of activation during 'Telepathy" by Sean Harribance & Gerrard Senehi, especially when the specific electromagnetic & cellular characteristics are considered, suggests the Parahippocampal region may be a focus of the mechanisms by which these Telepathic phenomena occur."

The study must be pursued by other researchers to confirm the patterns of brain circuitry in *the Parahippocampal region of brains of people engaged in effective Telepathy and the control samples not engaged in the phenomenon through experimentation on large scale. If the same pattern happens to come up at each experiment in the brain of a telepathic person and the pattern is not seen in the control sample person, then, we would have established that this area of the brain really does the processing of Telepathy.*

The Telepathic person's brain demonstratedsignificant activation of the right parahippocampal gyrus during a successful performance of a telepathic task. The comparison subject, who did not show any telepathic ability, demonstrated significant activation of the left inferior frontal gyrus. Conclusions: The findings of this study are suggestive of a limbic basis for telepathy and warrant further systematic research."

The brain part Parahippocampal region may be very important in researching Telepathy. I hope the neuroscience researchers along with medical counterparts jointly withParapsychological researchers will pursue this line of research

The following figure gives the location of this part in the human brain:

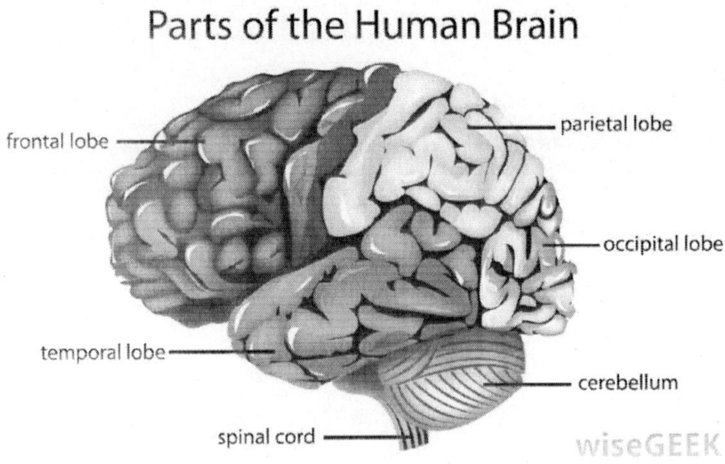

Picture showing position of Temporal lobe of the brain where Parahippocampal cortex lies. Source: *wisegreek.com/what-is-the-parahippocampal-gyrus.htm*

The exact location of this part of the temporal Lobe is presented in the following picture:

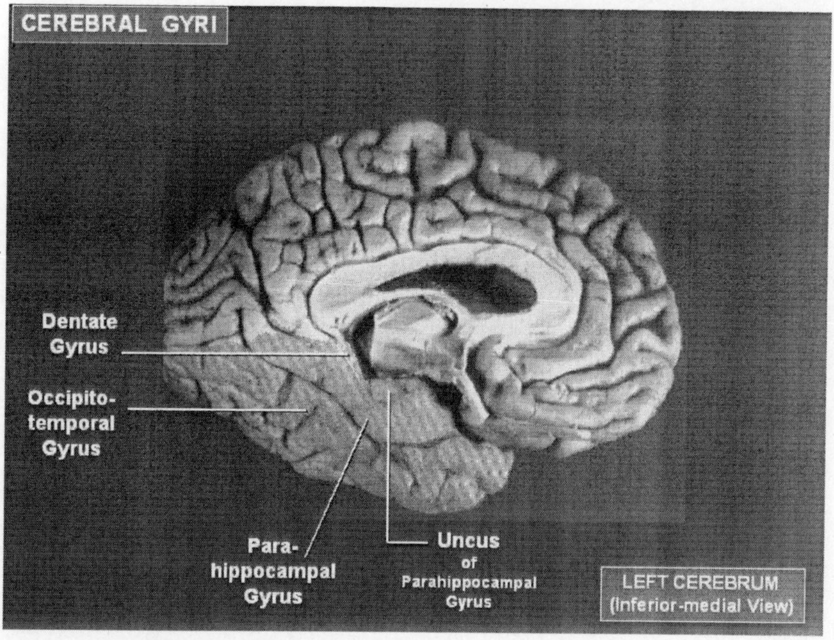

Picture showing the exact location of Para-hippocampal Gyrus and its Uncus in the Temporal lobe.
Source: infogalactic.com/info/parahippocampal_gyrus

Could neuroscience researchers pursue systematic research on the limbic basis for telepathy as suggested by authors? Who knows the secret lies in brain research? We all know that a major portion of the brain is still unexplored and the advancement in brain research taking a cue from the above findings may lead us to the discovery of the causes behind Telepathy. Neuroscience researchers must join hands with Parapsychological researchers to pursue Telepathy research pursuing this line of thinking.

Another approach is outlined by ***Dewey Catlin*** (2015):

"Your nervous system is composed of cells called neurons, which communicate with each other using chemical signals called neurotransmitters. When a neuron receives one of these signals, it generates a tiny electrical spike. And because millions of these signals are required for everything your brain does — clicking your mouse, reading this text, remembering breakfast, you name it — your brain is basically sending off pinpricks of electrical energy all the time.

The cool thing about this, of course, is that scientists can measure and map this electrical activity using existing technologies like EEG and fMRI machines. And once they have enough maps, they can begin to read them — a point that neuroscientists and researchers are just now approaching.

At the University of California at Berkeley, a team of cognitive scientists has managed to reconstruct clips of movies their subjects were watching, based solely on measurements of their brainwaves. "You could not see the close-up details," wrote the theoretical physicist Michio Kaku after watching one of the "movies," "[but] you could clearly identify the kind of object you were seeing."

How could we not only "read" a mind but also get that pattern of electrical signals into someone else's head?

There are invasive options; i.e., implanting some kind of device in your brain. In 2013, scientists at Duke University implanted two lab rats with microelectrode arrays and taught one of the rats to press one of two levers. Afterward, the second rat, who had not been trained, also seemed to know which level to push: It had received neural signals from the first rat, via the implant.

Recently, researchers have also had some luck with a non-invasive technique called transcranial magnetic stimulation, or TMS. When you put on a TMS headset it generates a magnetic field over your scalp, which can be used to activate neural pathways. Last fall, test subjects in India were able to use TMS to "think" the words "hola" and "ciao" to test subjects in France; the process was painfully slow, however, and the words weren't sent in their entirety — they had to be encoded as binary digits, uploaded to the Internet, sent, downloaded and then decoded as flashes of light. (WHEW.)

This is, while promising, a really clunky system. It's unsophisticated (no one has yet "sent" an actual emotion or idea), it's inexact (the rat still chose the wrong lever sometimes), and it's slower than virtually every other form of modern communication, save perhaps snail mail. These experiments also required access to some very expensive, sophisticated equipment. Even if you wanted to, you could not try this at home.

"Telepathy' technology remains so crude that it's unlikely to have any practical impact," wrote Mark Harris at the MIT Technology Review.

That said, these are only the very earliest days of telepathy research, and new developments are in the works. Among other things, researchers are looking into handheld, cell-phone-sized MRI machines that would make it easier and cheaper to capture your own brain activity. And the Army is developing a telepathy helmet, almost like a VR headset, that would condense and simplify all this electrical signal-sending — although that, experts say, is still decades away.

Decades are not a long-time span and hopefully, brain scanning devices will get developed which will make it possible to receive and decode neural activities arising out of Thought Signals to get thought transference possible without the use of the existing five senses, i.e., we would have accessed the Telepathic ability.

Summarizing the few possible approaches in future research which could be taken to understand Telepathy

- Thought Camera (Tesla's dream) could be developed by Physicists/ Engineers which could illuminate the images created by thoughts on the retina and transfer these illuminated images on external PCs to get an image corresponding to thoughts. The learnings can then be used by Neuroscientists to develop the capability of thought reading in the brain of each of us.

- Ralph Lewis; Venkatasubramanian Ganesan jointly with Jayakumar Peruvumba, Nagendra Hongasandra, Nagaraja Dindagur, Deeptha R, Gangadhar Bangalore; Michael Persinger & Kevin S Saroka; and Dewey Catlin, all suggest that Telepathy is correlated with a pattern formed in the *Parahippocampal region of the brain during the telepathic phenomenon.*

  This knowledge could help us to lead to an approach that each thought represented by patterns in form of complex connections between large arrays of neurons in the Pbrain could be accessed and could be transferred by creating the same pattern in the receiver's *Parahippocampal region of the brain* and then the receiver's brain would be able to decode the thought and understand the thought as sent by the sender. It seems the most plausible approach which is likely to succeed even faster than the thought camera. Medicine Researchers, Neuroscientists, and Physicists must work together and even involve a Parapsychologist to unravel the mystery. Not only unravel but make the brain capable to create the same patterns of an array of neurons instantaneously (in the receiver's brain) as originated in the sender's brain. Neuroscience has advanced to find a location in the brain where the thoughts get processed—only we have to identify the pattern of arrays of neurons and synapses created by thought and simulate a similar pattern to the other brain in the same location. It will be tricky but it will be done in a matter of decades by the researchers.

- Another approach is by creating algorithms - ***Matthews Hutson*** suggests that scientists have created the first algorithm of its kind to interpret- and accurately

reproduce— images seen or imagined by another person. It might be decades before the technology is ready for practical use, but researchers are one step closer to building systems that could help us project our inner mind's eye outward. Researchers have created movie clips, photos, and even dream imagery by matching brain activity to activity recorded earlier when viewing images. But these methods have all their limits: some deal with only narrow domains like face shapes, and others can't build an image from scratch—instead they must select from pre-programmed images or categories like "person" or "bird". This new work can generate recognizable images on the fly and even reproduce the shapes that are not seen, but imagined.
He is hopeful that with better measurements in algorithms, we might someday communicate thru mental pictures.
The algorithmic approach seems to be in the infancy stage and will have to cover a lot of ground before it is able to unravel Telepathic mysteries but the approach is commendable and cannot be brushed aside. Maybe the final breakthroughs emerge from this line of research, so it must be pursued by mathematical model makers, Physicists, and Neuroscientists.

There can be many more approaches, and all the approaches will certainly end up in making human beings capable of reading thoughts in other's minds—it is only a matter of a few decades!!

Till we make headway into the causal telepathic research using the above approaches coupled with more that are not covered above, we shall have to keep our fingers crossed!!

We, now, take up the next aspect of parapsychology—Clairvoyance in the next chapter.

Chapter 3

Clairvoyance/Remote viewing- on the rational pedestal

I took a trip on one of the fishing boats in Hawai and on the boat was a boy about 12 years old. While having a conversation with him I mentioned that I was writing a book on psychic principles and immediately he narrated his own incident—he told me that a month ago when his father died on the island of Oahu, a few hundred miles away, he knew it and ran in and told his mother, " Mom, papa is dead. I saw him and talked to him." His father's death was later confirmed by long-distance phone. ...The little boy had a ***clairvoyant vision*** *of his father, who appeared to him and said, 'Goodbye'.*

(*Dr. Joseph Murphy, (2014) in his book, Psychic Perception*)

The term Clairvoyance comes from two French terms which mean "Clear Vision". Clairvoyance/ Remote viewing is the ability of the mind to break the barrier of the normal perception of seeing through eyes and perceiving things without using eyes. In other words, these require seeing through the mind's eye.

Clairvoyance or remote viewing is seeing through the mind's eye over long distances. Irwin H J views Clairvoyance as a person's awareness of sensorially inaccessible visual events. Another school of thought thinks that Clairvoyance is an acute insight or perceptiveness that enables you to see objects or events that cannot be perceived by the physical senses in the form of mental imagery and intuition. An individual is described as "Clairvoyant" when he or she demonstrates keen perception or heightened senses. They can detect things that are not easily detected by the senses, and are even said to be able to see the future. The dictionary meaning of Clairvoyance---Clairvoyant is a person who claims that they are able to see into the future or communicate mentally with people who are dead or far away –the adjective is Clairvoyance which means the ability to see into the future.

We are not talking about clairvoyance as described in the dictionary—the aspects covered in dictionary meaning are dealt with in our discussions under the heads precognition and after-death communication (ADC).

We restrict Clairvoyance to exhibit an ability to see through the mind's eye i.e., we have visual perception without the use of normal visual perception through the eyes.

If we hear through the mind's ears i.e hearing perception occurs without the use of normal hearing perception through ears, the phenomenon is termed, "***Clairaudience***". To elaborate this, I cite here an incident: Dr. Murphy, (2014) narrates a real-life incident, *" One day about six months ago, a friend of mine wrote me, saying that he was driving the car along the highway to San Francisco when suddenly he heard his father's voice in his ear, saying, 'Son, pray for me. I have had a massive heart attack'. He pulled over as he could to the side of the road, stopped the car, and prayed for his father, affirming, "The peace of God rules in my father's heart. God is healing him now and God watches over him now and God watches over him.' He said that he silently prayed like this for about half an hour and suddenly felt a great sense of peace.*

Hearing the father's voice from a long distance (use of ear is not possible for long-distance) was through the mental capability of ***Clairaudience.***

Incidents depicting clairvoyance or clairaudience are bizarre but are happening sporadically and spontaneously across the world from time immemorial.

In Indian Epic Mahabharata, the blind king Dhritrashtra gets narration of the battlefield from his chariot driver Sanjay who was gifted with Clairvoyant/ Remote viewing capability. Sanjay could see the happenings at the battlefield sitting in the distantly located palace and narrated each event to the blind king.

We talked about Clairvoyance happening in ancient times of Mahabharata, during current times the most famous Clairvoyant was Mr. Croiset-***ESP Researchers forum*** **(2008)** in an article "ESP Researchers" describe feats of Croiset as follows:

The Netherlands' Gerard Croiset (1909–1980) was claimed to be a gifted clairvoyant. Perhaps the most remarkable of the many experiments conducted with Croiset was an endless series of chair tests that had been devised for him by Professor Tenhaeff of the Dutch Society for Psychical Research. From the outset of the tests in October of 1947, the results were startling and Croiset repeated the experiment several hundred times in front of scientists in five European nations.

The test itself was conducted quite simply. Croiset was taken to a theatre, an auditorium, or a meeting house, where a chair number was selected completely at random by a disinterested third party. Croiset then predicted, anywhere from one hour to 26 days, who would sit in the chair. The descriptions are given by the paragons (as such sensitives are called in Holland) were never vague and generalized but quite exact and astonishingly detailed. Often, not only was the individual's appearance described but also characteristics of his or her personality and even certain emotional difficulties that the subject may have been experiencing at the time. Sometimes Croiset saw the subject's past and was able topredict things about the person's future.

In June of 1964, Croiset was consulted in the murder case of the three Mississippi civil rights workers, James Chaney, Andrew Goodman, and Michael Schwerner. Via transatlantic telephone wire, Croiset accurately described the area where the three young men's bodies would be found and correctly implicated the local law enforcement officers as participants in the slayings. Although the FBI later made no formal acknowledgment of the clairvoyant's aid in the case, according to writer Jack Harrison Pollack, the federal agents actively sought information from the Utrecht sensitive."

Apart from the incidents involving an individual, there is a practical application of clairvoyants engaged in the government-sponsored project. The real-life application of remote viewing capability was made by US government for their defence usage for spying on enemy army installation. The Star Gate used the informational psi program, using the remote viewing method, was tasked on a total of 504 separate military and intelligence missions by a variety of agencies that required 2865 individual remote viewings to accomplish those stated missions. The data from these sessions produced actionable intelligence such that, of the 19 client agencies from 1973–1995, 17 were returning customers for the RV-HUMINT (remote viewing human intelligence) collection product—an 89% customer return rate. It seems highly unlikely that there would be such a high customer return rate if the RV-HUMINT-derived information was not worthy of such attention. (May& Marwaha, 2019).

We discussed the incidents from historical ancient times and from recent times. Such incidents keep on happening since ancient times. Ancient Hindu religious texts speak of Clairvoyance skills that can be accomplished through personal discipline and meditation.

Even western religions have records of people experiencing clairvoyance vision as cited in The Bible when Peter, James, and John "saw" a kingdom of God coming to the earth.

For centuries, clairvoyants learned to keep their experiences quiet for fear of being condemned as a witch

and the study of Clairvoyance started in a structured way only with the formation of the Society for Psychical Research in UK in the year 1882.

During the rise in popularity of spiritualists in the late 19th century, many psychics claimed to have the ability to see with the mind.

The Marquis de Puysegur took inspiration from Franz Mesmer - who theorized that there were forces of energy called animal magnetism. In 1784 he was treating a local dull-witted peasant named Victor Race. During treatment, Race reportedly would go into trance and undergo a personality change, becoming fluent and articulate, and giving diagnosis and prescription for his own disease as well as those of others. When he came out of the trance state, he would be unaware of anything he had said or done. He was reportedly the first to use the term "clairvoyance".

Early scientific attempts to test the ability, by the likes of chemist Williams Gregory, saw participants who were asked to identify a concealed image.

Clairvoyance was a reported ability of some mediums during the spiritualist period of the late 19th and early 20th centuries and was one of the phenomena studied by members of the Society for Psychical Research (SPR). Psychics of many descriptions have claimed clairvoyant ability up to the present day.

Around 1910, Stanford University entered into psychical research, studying Clairvoyance and Psychokinesis under stringent laboratory conditions.

Later, in the 1920s, the Parapsychology Laboratory of Duke University entered the field, led by J.B. Rhine (1894-1980). Rhine believed that psychical research should be moved out from societies doing the research and brought it into laboratories in university and changed the research to experimental science. Rhine undertook experiments that followed the scientific methods of other disciplines (e.g., using quantitative data & statistical analysis).

While Rhine was doing pioneering work on clairvoyance, there appear to be instances of other researchers engaged in researching Clairvoyance. Irwin H J (1999) gives an account of Ina Jephson of the Society of psychic research doing sizeable card-guessing experiments during 1924-1928. The investigation of the results of these experiments, she claimed, supported the hypothesis of clairvoyance.

Rhine's card-guessing experiments were done using specially designed Zener Cards. Using these cards, he set up experimental techniques for testing clairvoyance in the laboratory. Several experiments were done using methodology —One card every minute would be removed from Deck and placed with face down and the participant was asked to guess the shape (out of 5 shapes in Zener cards) and if the guess was correct it was taken as a "hit". This ability of correct guessing above chance probability was considered an extrasensory ability. This ability was found in several people during extensive experiments done by the laboratory. Details are available in a book by Rhine. However, subsequently, other researchers could not replicate his results and his line of research did not make much headway after him.

Clairvoyance / Remote viewing was later examined by what is called ***Ganzfeld*** Experiments. Translucent ping-pong ball halves are taped over the eyes and headphones are placed over the ears; a red floodlight directed toward the eyes produces an undifferentiated visual field, and white noise played through the headphones produces an analogous auditory field. It is this homogeneous perceptual environment that is called the *Ganzfeld* ('total field'). To reduce internal somatic 'noise,' the receiver typically also undergoes a series of progressive relaxation exercises at the beginning of the Ganzfeld period. A visual stimulus (art print, photograph, or brief videotaped sequence) is randomly selected from a large pool of such stimuli to serve as the target for the session and the receiver is asked to view it with mind's eye and later told to make sketches as per his mental visualization. The sketches having a close resemblance to the pictures presented as a stimulus are taken as hits and the results are evaluated statistically to infer whether the probability is above chance level.

The ganzfeld technique indicates that information can be exchanged mentally after the receiver is placed in an altered state of consciousness (the ganzfeld).

The remote viewing experiment, in one of its many forms, investigates whether information can be gained without requiring a special altered state, and without a sender. For example, in one type of remote viewing experiment, a pool of several hundred photographs is created. One of these is randomly selected by a third party to be the target, and it is set aside in a remote location. The experimental participant then attempts to sketch or otherwise describe that remote target photo. This is repeated for a total of say, 7 different targets. Many ways of evaluating the results of this test have been developed, including some highly sophisticated methods. One common (and easy) method is to take the group of seven target photos and responses, randomly shuffle the targets and responses, and then ask independent judges to rank order or match the correct targets with the participant's actual responses. If there was a real transfer of information, the responses should correspond more closely to the correct targets than to the mismatched targets.

Several thousand such trials have been conducted by dozens of investigators over the past 25 years, involving hundreds of participants. The cumulative database strongly indicates that information about remote photos, actual scenes, and events can be perceived. Some of these experiments have also been used to successfully study precognition by having a participant describe a photo that would be randomly selected in the future. (Parapsychological Association, 2011).

Laboratory experiments by Rhine and subsequent Ganzfeld experiments were done extensively to prove that there is substantial evidence to prove that the psi happenings were not due to chance cause (as size effects were found pointing this) but were in fact real anomalous incidents. Meta-analysis was done to pool several studies and these led to prove the positive statistical significance of the existence of clairvoyance / remote viewing capability.

While on one side pro-clairvoyance research was gaining popularity and clairvoyance sporadic and spontaneous events were happening across the globe; on the other hand, several ambitious people wanted to make name and fame in a short time by adopting fraudulent means by staging shows for claiming capabilities of clairvoyance and, also, there arose learned skeptics who presented their research work opposing the psychic phenomena including Clairvoyance.

Rightly said by Wiseman Richards, Schlitz Marilyn, Dean Radin, and Watt Caroline (2006): "For well over a hundred years scientists have explored the possible existence of psychic ability (Edge, Morris, Palmer, & Rush, 1986). This work has generated considerable controversy, with proponents arguing that the cumulative research supports the existence of such abilities (see, e.g. Bem & Honorton, 1994; Utts, 1991) and skeptics claiming that the evidence suffers from possible methodological or statistical problems(see, e.g. Alcock, 2003; Hyman, 1994). Researchers on both sides of the debate have tended to collaborate with colleagues who share similar beliefs about the existence ofpsychic ability."

The above paper dwelt on the collaborative efforts of proponents and the skeptics and there emerged interesting findings. We shall discuss the same later; first, let us see what skeptics have to say about clairvoyance / remote viewing.

We first take up Richard Wiseman's study on Clairvoyance / Remote viewing:

Guy Lyon Playfair (2014) mentions the study by Richard Wiseman *"Hot on the heels of Messrs. Moulton and Kosslyn (see MediaWatch: Neuroimaging Used in Attempts to Resolve the Psi Debate), along comes Richard Wiseman, describing in New Scientist (10 June 2009) his latest publicity stunt under the modest title "Tweeting my way to a scientific breakthrough". Results, according to an editorial, 'fail to show any support for the paranormal'. They do indeed, as one does not have to be psychic to have predicted, for this was clearly another of those experiments that are designed to come up with negative results and reassure the general public that psi is a load of rubbish. They also fail to show any sign of what is usually understood to be a breakthrough.*

It purported to be a mass experiment in remote viewing (RV), or clairvoyance (seeing at a distance), with the participation of some 1,000-plus 'twitterers'. For the first informal test, Wiseman went to a location and asked people to tweet their impressions of what he was looking at. He then sent out details of where to find a photo of where he was so that twitterers received feedback within twenty minutes or so. He reports, somewhat vaguely, that what he calls, without defining them, 'paranormal believers' claimed 'high levels of correspondence between their thoughts and the actual locations', but gives no examples and no statistics.

Oh well, this was only an informal test.

The subsequent formal one ran for four days and was designed to test 'whether the group as a whole was psychic' and whether believers did better than disbelievers. As before, Wiseman went somewhere and asked participants to send in their thoughts and impressions. They were then shown five photos, one of which was of the target location, and asked to choose which one it was. Their choices were pooled and the photo receiving the most votes was designated as their collective choice. As you will have guessed, the group got it wrong four times out of four, enabling Wiseman to conclude that 'the study didn't support the existence of remote viewing', adding patronizingly that 'it suggests that those who believe in the paranormal are simply good at finding illusory correspondences between their thoughts and a target – which is maybe why they believe in the first place.'

Prima facie, the impression given is that there is evidence that the phenomenon of remote viewing is not possible and there is collective evidence pointing this.

- The same paper says that deeper analysis of the case posits a contrary view arising out of the following observed facts from the case:
- We are not told exactly how many people took part and what percentage of the individual impressions was correct. If, as Wiseman seems to imply, nobody made a single statement that could apply to the target location, this would be a result of some significance.
- We are not told how many individuals, if any, guessed all four targets correctly.
- The implication that if the group as a whole failed to demonstrate collective clairvoyance, therefore clairvoyance does not exist, is as absurd as asking randomly chosen people to play a scale on a tuba regardless of whether they had any previous experience of tuba playing, or indeed any musical ability at all, and concluding that the evidence for tuba-playing ability is so weak as to be insignificant.
- One reader whose views deserve respect, Professor Brian Josephson, made a similar point – any accurate remote viewing in the group would have been lost in a combination of noise from those not having those skills, and systematic error'. It would have been better, he added politely, 'if the experimenter had discussed methodological issues with experts in the field before starting the experiment'.

Normally, the skeptics argue that experiments on clairvoyance are weak in design and hence sensory leakages are possible and the bizarre astounding results obtained could be due to weak experimental design. The same logic of weakness in experimental design holds true for the above experiment by a skeptic as well.

The above experiment was a sincere attempt for testing the Clairvoyance / remote-viewing phenomenon. On other extreme end are instances where a deliberate attempt is made by a person claiming to possess clairvoyant/ remote viewing capability using fraudulent means.

Normally it is assumed that since the usually happening clairvoyant events are spontaneous, these cannot be fraudulent because perpetration of fraud needs planning and in such spontaneous cases there is no time available for planning. But there are instances when a trickster pretends manifestation (with pre-planning of course) of a spontaneous clairvoyant event before a gathering of people in the show staged by him. Irwin H J (1999) describes the possibility of such an incident in his book, I reproduce the same here below:

"One technique is called *Billet reading* and is useful for performance before a large group. Members of the audience are each invited to write on a card the name of a loved one and a short description of some distinctive characteristic of that person. Each card is sealed in an envelope by each person and passed on to the "Psychic" who then selects envelopes at random to read using clairvoyance capability. After reading a card clairvoyantly, the envelope is opened, the card is read to the audience to establish the accuracy of the clairvoyant attempt, and the person who wrote the card is asked to acknowledge its authenticity. The mentalist proceeds through several cards in this fashion with great success and the audience's donations are gratefully received to support the good work. How is this performance achieved by sleight of hand?

The trick is fiendishly simple. A pre-scripted name and characteristic are read out clairvoyantly (which is not there in the card held by the psychic) and a stooge in the audience acknowledges its accuracy on opening the envelope. Since the card is not shown to the audience, they assume that the card belonged to the stooge. The psychic sees the picked up the first card, memorizes the content and puts it away and takes the second envelope and before opening announces the contents which he had read and looks for person in the audience who had written it and certainly there is one who gets up to acknowledge its authenticity. While getting acknowledgment he opens the envelope as proof and reads the next message and keeps it away and reads this message as a clairvoyant message for next, and he goes on predicting correct answers presumably by clairvoyance. After few cases, the audience becomes convinced about his clairvoyant capability."

This reminds me of my childhood when I used to play a magic trick to our friends using playing cards. I used to tell our friends that they will have to just tell me the first top card from the deck and then I can tell each card with its face down and without looking at them. The deck of cards was taken and was pointed towards the friends. The first card was reversed and put on top of the deck which was so held that the top reversed card was seen by the audience and the bottom-most card was facing me i.e., the topmost card was the only card that had a face-up and the rest had face down so that I could see the bottom-most card without anyone knowing about it. After the audience read out the card facing them, I will take the deck to my back and pretend to chant some mantras and will be taking the bottom-most card and reverse it and place it at top of the deck and show it audience and shall announce the card (I had seen it as the bottom-most card while they saw the first card); while announcing I shall be seeing the now bottom-most card which is facing me and the trick will continue and I shall be reading all the cards supposedly clairvoyantly. Amusing isn't it? The Psychic did play the same childish magic differently!!

It is irony of fate that such tricksters were instrumental in dimming the credibility of the Clairvoyance phenomenon. People, naturally, suspected foul play even in genuine clairvoyant cases.

Bizarre as the clairvoyant incidents are, people find it difficult to accept them and they would be looking for some clue, some pretext, some excuse which could help them prove these as mere hoaxes or figs of imagination or could point to some sensory leakages which could result in their manifestation.

Wiseman while doing the above study (that we discussed) had started by conceding the factuality and correctness of the Clairvoyant project, "Stargate" undertaken by US army. Later he himself cast a doubt on the clairvoyant capability of a member of the team who was supposed to be a star clairvoyant.

Guy Lyon Playfair (2014) brings out this point very well in his paper:

"Wiseman prefaces his report with a brief reference to the U.S. Army's Stargate project, which trained military remote viewers and used them for nearly twenty years. 'Some have claimed that results supported [RV's] existence', he conceded. They have indeed – the U.S.Army for example, which awarded one of its longest-serving viewers, Joe McMoneagle, the Legion of Merit. This is given for 'exceptionally meritorious conduct in the performance of outstanding services and achievements, and Joe's citation credited him with 'producing crucial and vital intelligence unavailable from any other source'. Quite an impressive claim, you might think.

Wiseman, as it happens, has met McMoneagle and witnessed an experiment he carried out some years ago at the Rhine Research Center in Durham, NC., so he knows perfectly well how Remote Viewing is done properly having seen for himself. After Joe had made a drawing of a target location, the thirty attendees were shown the usual five photos of possible sites and 29 of them picked the right one. Wiseman then complained that the controls were not tight enough, so McMoneagle invited him to take over the protocol and run it any way he liked the following day, which he duly did. Joe still got 29 first-place matches out of thirty. Not surprisingly, as Joe notes in his book

The Stargate Chronicles (p.251), 'Richard has refused to discuss it since."

The subject of clairvoyance has remained debatable even when the incidences are happening and we witness the same with astonishment. How strongly the views against can be presented is demonstrated below:

"Anyone can throw out strings of words or sentences or draw pictures that other people can find meaningful and apparently clairvoyant. This fact, however, is irrelevant to establishing that clairvoyance is real. Subjective validation and selective thinking, *acting in concert with wishful thinking,* ignorance of cognitive biases, *and occasional fraud can account for the widespread belief in the reality of clairvoyance. (Depending on which poll one cites, between 25% and 40% of us believe that clairvoyance is real.)*

Attempts by scientists to establish the reality of clairvoyance have been going on since the middle of the 19th century. So far, the overwhelming bulk of the evidence indicates that clairvoyance does not exist.' (skepdic.com/clairvoyance.html)

The last line posits a strong view against Clairvoyance being real but admits a fact that there exists some evidence that the phenomenon could be real. This is clear if you study the last sentence critically- I repeat the sentence for you to examine-"*So far, the overwhelming* ***bulk of the evidence*** *indicates that clairvoyance does not exist"*. The words made bold clearly indicate that there exists some evidence which is suggestive that the clairvoyance phenomena are real.

While the above article leaves a doubt that Clairvoyance is not real, there are skeptics who strongly believe that Psychical ability (including Clairvoyance) does not exist. In fact, James Randi, a magician, has offered $ 1000000 to anyone who can demonstrate psychic powers under controlled conditions and no one, as yet, could stake the claim successfully.

James Randi, who has tested many people who think they have psychic abilities, has found that when he has tested the alleged paranormal powers of psychics

1. they had never before tested their powers under controlled conditions, and
2. those who don't offer preposterous rationalizations for their inability to perform seem genuinely baffled at their failure.

Often, psychics are not frauds; they genuinely believe in their powers. But they've never tested their powers in any meaningful way. (*skepdic.com/psychic.html).*

Whatever be the arguments against psychics, psychics are still popular. Why they are popular and the tricks played by them to gain popularity are well brought out in a paper by Todd Carroll(1994)- The main reasons for belief in such paranormal powers as clairvoyance and clairaudience are

(1) the perceived accuracy of psychic predictions and readings;
(2) the seemingly uncanny premonitions which many people have, especially in dreams; and
(3) the seemingly fantastic odds against such premonitions or predictions being correct by coincidence or chance.

Most believers do not base their conviction on the scientific evidence for psi, which is claimed to be overwhelming by Dean Radin.

However, the accuracy of psychic predictions is grossly overrated. The belief in the accuracy of clairvoyants such as Edgar Cayce and Jeanne Dixon is due to several factors, including mass media error and hype. For example, it has been repeatedly reported in the mass media that Jeanne Dixon predicted the assassination of President Kennedy. She did not. The *New York Times* helped spread the myth that Edgar Cayce transformed from an illiterate into a healer when hypnotized."

The most frequently used trick by the fraudulent psychics is "hot readings" i.e., they have hard information about you that they have gained through a variety of surreptitious methods. They may have done research on you and that's why they know things they shouldn't know. They may have an accomplice who acts as a decoy in the audience to support your clairvoyant feat- "Billet reading" that we discussed in the above paragraphs is an apt example. The psychic himself/herself may chat you up before the reading and get information from you that he/she can use later. Still, others are magicians who try to pass off their conjuring skills as paranormal powers.

Equally popular is "cold reading" which is used to camouflage the psychic abilities- a guide to cold reading is provided in the paper by Todd Carroll cited above:

"Guide to Cold Reading that is usually followed by pretending psychics:

1. *You must do your research. You have to be up on the latest statistics (e.g., most plane crashes are in April; most planes have something red on their tails). You have to know what people, in general, are like from polls and surveys. Also, you must pick up in casual conversation before a performance any information that might be useful later.*
2. *You must convince the mark that he or she will be the reason for success or failure. This is actually true because it is the mark who will provide all the vital information that seems so shocking and revealing. It is human nature to find meaning, so this is not a difficult chore. The mark will bring significance to much of what you throw at him or her. If you bring up "June" and get no response, you make the mark feel like they're not remembering properly. If you say "8, the 8th month, 8-years, August" and somebody bites by saying "Dad died in August" and the mark thinks it was you who told her*

that fact rather than the other way around. When you say "I see a watch, a bracelet, something on the wrist" and the mark says "I put my necklace in mom's casket." You say "Right. She thanks you for it, too." Everybody thinks you knew she put a necklace in the casket and they will forget that you were fishing for some jewelry on the wrist.

3. *Be observant. Does the person have expensive jewelry on but worn-out clothes? Is she wearing a pin with the letter 'K' on it? (You better know that 'Kevin' is a good guess here. But it doesn't matter, really. Since, when the mark tells you the name of the person, she'll think you are the one who told her the name!)*
4. *Use flattery and pretend you know more than you do.*

The list goes on, but you get the idea. What looks like psychic power is little more than a game of Twenty Questions, or a fishing expedition, with the mark providing all the relevant details and connecting all the dots, while the "psychic" appears to be getting messages from beyond (by Psychic powers). Of course, sometimes the "psychic" is simply an observant, thoughtful person, who says things appropriate for the age and gender of the subject."

General sweeping remarks, open-ended statements, and double-meaning phrases are generally effectively used by the pretending psychics/clairvoyants to prove their paranormal capabilities when none exist.

Such deceptive staged clairvoyant feats do open up possibilities of fair criticism of parapsychological aspects including clairvoyance.

Alcock James (2013) admits being a critic of parapsychology and he goes on to say: *"I have myself long been a critic of parapsychological research, and it is only fair that I state my views 'upfront. I have yet to find any empirical evidence that persuades me that it is likely that paranormal phenomenaactually exist. Moreover, I am well aware of just how often our brains can mislead us and can lead us to believe that we have had a paranormal experience evenwhen no such thing has happened. Indeed, even if there is no such thing as a paranormal phenomenon, human information processing works in such a way that weare all likely from time to time to have experiences that seem for all the world to be paranormal. For me as a psychologist, these experiences themselves — the reports of extrasensory perception and the like — are fascinating in their own right, even if, as I presume, they are not paranormal, for they can tell us a great deal about how our brains work and about our beliefs and needs and expectations if we are willing to listen."*

Discussion so far is hung in balance-one one side there are real sporadic spontaneous clairvoyance incidents backed by credible laboratory card-guessing and ganzfeld experiments which have results probability of which were found above chance levels. Also, the Star Gate program was a real-life application of clairvoyance / remote viewing application. On the flip side are the incidents which are proved fraudulent through ingenious magical/psychological tricks and there are strong skeptic views claiming faulty designs in experiments leading to sensory leakage which bring down the credibility of experiments; and where design faults are not found, skeptics claim that clairvoyant incident must be by chance or synchronicity may be at play or the positive results may be due to experimenter effect. Arguments on both sides are strong and no final conclusion can be drawn.

In such a scenario, I once again reiterate that answer can only be got by going in for causal research on Clairvoyance. We have seen that the proponents are only trying to prove through laboratory experiments that the probability of events happening is above chance level and hence clairvoyance are real. But I say that look around the sporadic spontaneous clairvoyant incidents which happen unannounced and there is no time for any planning so that fraud could be a possibility—such events are proof that the events are real and only if we do research to find out the root cause which makes these manifest, we would have uncovered the truth and then only we could be able to assert that it be considered a scientific phenomenon. I raised this point in my recent book-Parapsychology -trending towards causal research.

The possible approaches which could lead us to a meaningful causal Clairvoyance research were indicated in the book and these are pertinent here so I bring those in our discussions:

In the previous chapter, while discussing causal research for Telepathy, we learned that some neuroscience research papers indicated an area in the brain that gets activated when the Telepathic Process starts. Recalling it from Telepathy discussions-

The comparison of the pattern of circuitry in the Parahippocampal part of the brain of the person engaged in the successful accomplishment of Telepathy with the circuitry of the person not engaged in Telepathy had given an understanding about this location where Telepathy is getting processed in the brain.

On similar lines, if brain imaging is done of a person in process of accomplishing a successful Clairvoyance feat and comparing it with the brain images of a person not engaged in Clairvoyance could lead us to find the location where Clairvoyance gets processed. Maybe it is the same area as was for Telepathy—who knows?

In fact, most of the Brain research had progressed through a similar approach. When Neuro-physicians/ Neuro-researchers were faced with a patient having some psychological disorders, the brain imaging of the patient was compared with brain imaging of a healthy person to get an idea of what is different in the brain of the patient which is causing the trouble. This led to an understanding of the functioning of many parts of the brain and we enhanced our knowledge about what part of the brain does what?

Maybe this approach may shed light on brain circuitry responsible for the manifestation of Clairvoyance.

A study was done at Georgetown University Medical Centre by Neuro-researchers Amber Leaver, MS, Jennifer Van Lare, BS, Brandon Zielinski, Ph.D., and Andrea Halpern, Ph.D. (2009).

It could reveal brain activity linked to Anticipation activity-i.e the activity behind Clairvoyance:

Neuroscientists have, for the first time, shown what brain activity looks like when someone anticipates an action or sensory input that soon follows. They say this neural clairvoyance involves strong activity in areas of the brain responsible for preparing the body to move.

The findings were made by using functional magnetic resonance imaging (fMRI) in a group of student volunteers who brought with them favourite music CDs. The scientists examined brain images during the silence between songs and found it brimming with activity. Other students who listened to music they had never heard in sequence before did not have that same neural bustle.

The researchers found that during the anticipatory silence between the songs excitatory signals passed from the ***prefrontal cortex*** *to the nearby* ***premotor cortex****. The prefrontal cortex is the brain's "executive" centre, which plans and orchestrates complex cognitive behaviours. The premotor cortex and its associated systems, which include the basal ganglia and the cerebellum, are involved in preparing the body to act – perhaps to move or to sing. "*

The picture below gives the location of the Prefrontal Cortex and Primary motor cortex where the neural activation takes place during anticipatory Clairvoyant actions:

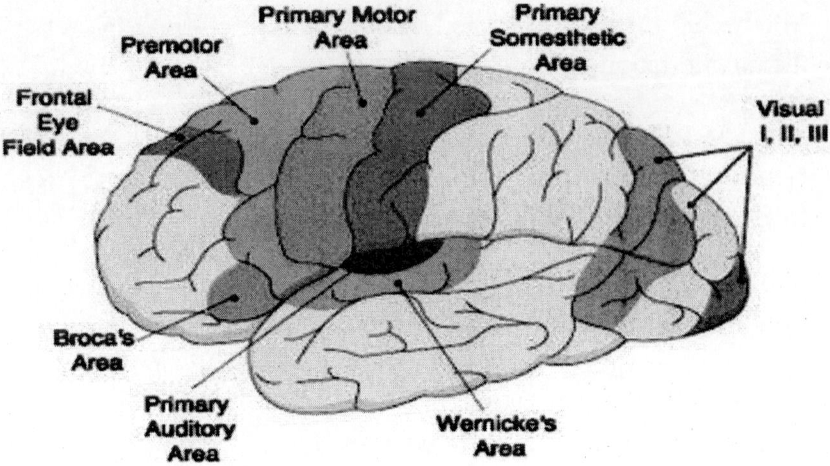

(Source- printerest.com/pin/825636544161574750/)

As we had a specific area for a neural activity for Telepathy, this may be the area for Clairvoyance.

Of course, more replications of the experiments must be done using Clairvoyance feats with a comparison with controls of non-clairvoyance activities before it is firmly established that the same patterns of circuitry happen when the Clairvoyance feats occur and the pattern is not the same in the control species.

The above observation does open a way towards the Causal Clairvoyance Research. If repeated experiments prove that Prefrontal Cortex and Premotor Cortex have a correlation with Clairvoyance, we shall have to understand the exact pattern of neural circuitry while clairvoyance is happening. This will be the first step towards Causal Clairvoyance Research.

The next steps to follow will be to understand how this pattern can be created at will. The brain mechanism is complex and the neuro-researchers together with Medical Researchers and Parapsychological Researchers should make efforts to have a deeper understanding of these brain areas and try to figure out the ways to create the needed circuitry at our will. Having done that the manifestation of

Clairvoyance feat will certainly manifest and a cause-effect relationship would get revealed.

Following this approach, who knows, we shall be able to unravel the mystery behind Clairvoyance.

There is another article published in 2011 which finds brain areas that had neural activities during the Clairvoyance feat of predicting the near future.

Science News (2011) brought the details: *"The researchers focused on the midbrain dopamine system (MDS), an evolutionarily ancient system that provides signals to the rest of the brain when unexpected events occur. Using functional MRI (fMRI), they found that this system encodes prediction error when viewers are forced to choose what will happen next in a video of an everyday event.*

Predicting the near future is vital in guiding behaviour and is a key component of theories of perception, language processing, and learning, says Jeffrey M. Zacks, Ph.D., WUSTL associate professor of psychology in Arts & Sciences and lead author of a paper on the study in a forthcoming issue of the Journal of Cognitive Neuroscience.

Zacks and his group were keenly interested in what the participants' brains were doing as they tried to predict a new event.

In the functional MRI experiment, Zacks and his colleagues saw significant activity in several midbrain regions, among them the ***substantia nigra*** *-- "ground zero for the dopamine signaling system" -- and in a set of nuclei called the* ***striatum****.*

The Brain

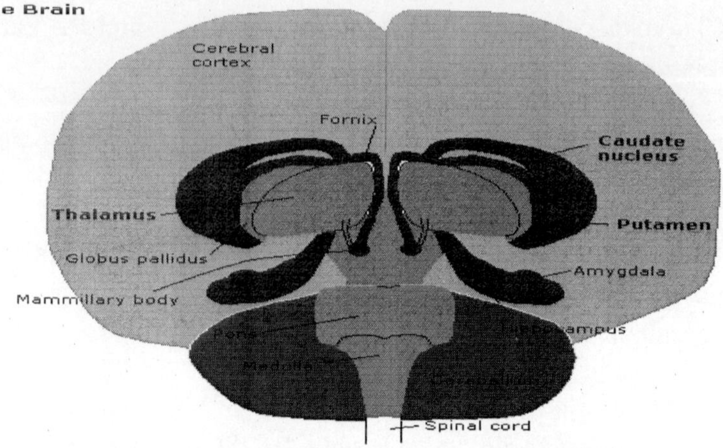

The brain as viewed from the underside and front. The thalamus and Corpus Striatum (Putamen, caudate and amygdala) have been splayed out to show detail.

Corpus Striatum

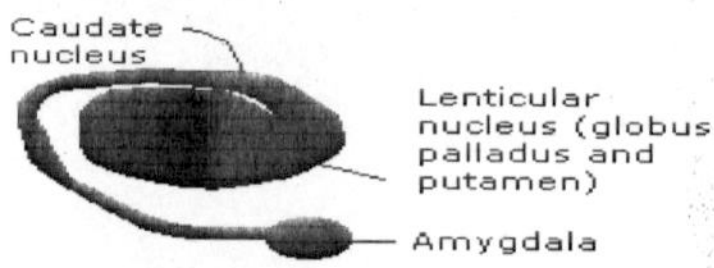

The substantia nigra, Zacks says, is the part of the brain hit hardest by Parkinson's disease, and is important for controlling movement and making adaptive decisions."

Pictures show Substantia Nigra and Striatum—the parts of the brain getting neuronal activation on getting Clairvoyant impulses

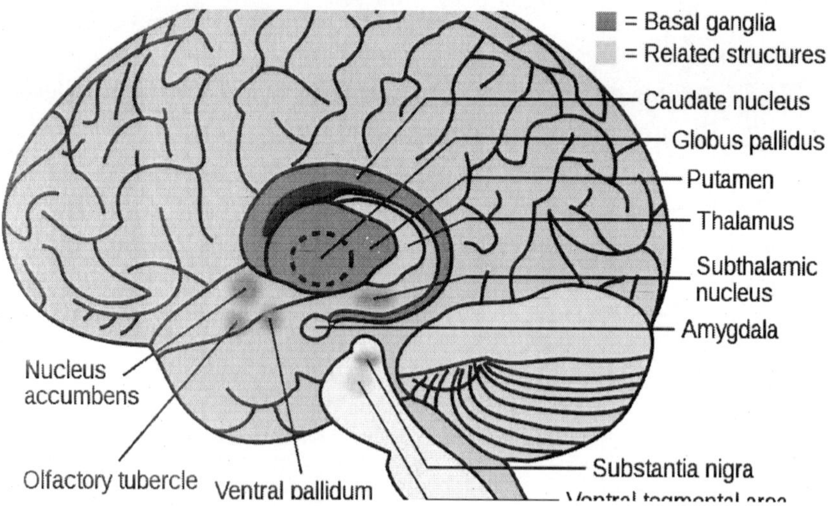

The above pictures give the location of Substantia Nigra and Striatum where we see neural activities when Clairvoyance phenomena are occurring. The experimental observation needs to be confirmed through extensive replications where brain imaging must be done for each Clairvoyance feat along with non-clairvoyance brain imaging to confirm that the patterns formed are uniquely related to clairvoyance. We realize that this is not easy to do but we can do experimentation in laboratories on mediums selected with prior experiences and designing experimentation of looking at distant pre-selected objects by the experimenter. Brain mapping must continue while experimentation is going on. The cases where a "hit" is recorded and where "hit" does not happen should be separated and the brain images must be compared. If patterns for hits are all alike and differ from the patterns during "Non-hits" would prove that activation of the brain in a particular fashion happens during successful clairvoyance. The pattern must be frozen as proof of a correlation between clairvoyance and brain activity.

The first step towards causal clairvoyance research would lead us to further headway and the researchers then must find out ways to simulate to achieve the particular neuronal pattern through other means which could be done at our own will. If this succeeds, we would have solved the mystery behind Clairvoyance.

Undoubtedly the above is easy to say but nearly impossible to do!! I am confident that the brain has achieved the impossible in past and will, one day, achieve this nearly impossible feat also!

As we saw Neuroscience has advanced to locate areas in the brain which get activated when telepathy or clairvoyance feats manifest. Further neuroscience research into this neuronal activation will certainly lead to give further hints for proceeding in causal research for telepathy and clairvoyance. I strongly appeal to Neuroscientists to take the research forward.

With the advancement of science, we shall one day arrive at the basic root cause which is responsible for the manifestation of Clairvoyance /remote viewing, and then and then only the phenomena will get acknowledged as becoming part of mainstream science.

We have taken a rational view of the phenomena giving equal importance to proponent and opponent views and have proposed a solution to the stalemate by going in for causal research. The author is confident that the key to the dilemma lies only in Causal Clairvoyance/Remote viewing Research.

In the next chapter, we shall discuss Precognition/ Premonition, another intriguing aspect of Parapsychology.

Chapter 4

Precognition/ Premonition- On rational pedestal

Just days before Lincoln was shot, he told his wife of a dream that he had: "He was woken up by the sound of crying and went into the East Room of the White House, where a casket was laid open. There was a throng of mourners as well as several men guarding the casket. When he asked who was in the casket, one of the soldiers told him that it was the President, who had been killed by an assassin." Three days after telling his wife this dream, Lincoln was shot and killed by JohnWilkesBooth.
(https://biography.yourdictionary.com/abraham.lincoln)

The ability to predict or have knowledge of something in advance of its occurrence is Precognition or Premonition. Precognition is the apparent ability to predict unexpected future events, and precognitive dreams are among the most commonly reported seemingly paranormal experiences. The precognition events are very common.

The instances depicting precognition keep on pouring from different parts of the world from time immemorial which baffles us because their perception does not happen through our known five senses.

The instances are so intriguing that the subject attracted cinema and we had a wonderful movie in India, "100 days" in which the heroine is gifted with the paranormal power of seeing the future and she could dream about future happenings in her life and those came true. On one occasion, she happens to dream about a famous sports magazine that has a picture of a horse on its cover page. When she contacted the editor of the magazine, she is informed that there has never been an issue having a horse on its cover page nor is there for future editions as for the next six months the cover page has been finalized. She, then, forgets this as a normal dream. But a month later while visiting a bookstall she sees the new edition of the magazine with a picture of a horse. She is stunned! She, then, contacted the editor and told her that she was informed that for the next 6 months the cover picture was final and the horse picture was not there in any future editions but the current edition does have a cover picture of a horse. The editor informed that they had to put this picture because the horse had done a remarkable feat in a recent famous race and it deserved the attention of people so they had to change the previous picture and replace it with a horse picture because the edition carried a story for that race. Remarkable isn't it!!

Above is a piece of fiction but people are observing such incidents in real life. Equally stunning are the real-life incidents, one of which is discussed by Caroline Watt (2017): *"Stevenson recounts the precognition of the sinking of the Titanic. A New York woman had a vivid dream on the night of the sinking, so striking that she woke her husband to tell him about it: "I just saw the mother in a crowded lifeboat rocking in the ocean swell" (Stevenson, 1960, p 157). The woman didn't know her mother was on the ship. Her mother had boarded at Southampton and had intended to surprise her daughter. Fortunately, she had indeed been saved by a lifeboat and eventually made it safely to New York."*

Caroline in the same paper brings about an account of a study concerning precognition: *"In the 1950s, W. E. Cox attempted to observe if there was any dip in passenger numbers on the days that a train was involved in an accident, compared to passenger numbers on the same journey on preceding days and weeks. Cox (1956) did indeed find a tendency for passenger numbers to be lower on trains that crashed – something Cox attributed to 'subliminal precognition', though in fact some of the passengers may have dreamt about the impending doom and consciously decided to avoid the journey.*

However, it's difficult to be sure that the dropped passenger numbers were due to conscious or unconscious precognition. For instance, another external factor such as bad weather might have both deterred passengers from traveling as well as contributing to a train wreck."

The subject matter, "Precognition" is being studied by researchers for a long time and the parapsychological researchers have been staking claims that their studies prove that precognition incidents are real. Let us take a brief journey into the history of Precognition:

History of research on Precognition: "Since ancient times, precognition has been associated with trance and dream states involved in phenomena such as prophecy, fortune-telling, and second sight, as well as waking premonitions. These phenomena were widely accepted and reports have persisted throughout history, with most instances appearing in dreams.

Such claims of seeing the future have never been without their skeptical critics. Aristotle carried out an inquiry into allegedly prophetic dreams in his *On Divination in Sleep*. He accepted that "it is quite conceivable that some dreams may be tokens and causes [of future events]" but also believed that "most [so-called prophetic] dreams are, however, to be classed as mere coincidences...". Where Democritus had suggested that emanations from future events could be sent back to the dreamer, Aristotle proposed that it was, rather, the dreamer's sense impressions that reached forward to the event. An early investigation into claims of precognition was published by the missionary Fr. P. Boilat in 1883. He claimed to have put an unspoken question to an African witch doctor whom he mistrusted. Contrary to his expectations, the witch doctor gave him the correct answer without ever having heard the question. (Source Wikipedia) An article which appeared on November 28, 2016, in The Psychic Life-Exploring the Spiritual Web gives a brief history of Precognition as follows:

The history of precognition or the ability to see into the future has been recognized since ancient times when seers, diviners, and mediums were regularly sought by kings and ordinary people alike for their access to the future.

However, scientific studies on the phenomena were not conducted until recently. It was British aeronautics engineer, J.W. Dunne who first conducted a systematic study on precognition after discovering that his dreams happened a few days after having them. Dunne began his study on precognition and discovered that he shared the same ability with numerous others. In 1927, he published his findings and theories in the book, "An Experiment with Time." He theorized that many people possess the ability of precognition, but this is not recognized due to failure to recall the dream or analyse the dream symbols properly.

Other studies followed Dunne's. The most sophisticated and systematic study on ESP and precognition at that time was done by J.B. Rhine at Duke University. Rhine, a psychologist, and his wife Louisa conducted experiments on ESP at the Parapsychology Laboratory at Duke University in the 1930s. This resulted in the largest compilation of dream evidence from thousands of accounts of ESP experiences available to research today.

J.A. Barker, an English psychiatrist, established the British Premonitions Bureau in 1967. This agency collected data using individuals who had precognitive abilities in order to gather early information about impending disasters. Another agency created in an attempt to study and use the knowledge gained from precognition was the Princeton Engineering Anomalies Research Lab, which spent years on research studies.

A parapsychologist Daryl Bem of Cornell University has demonstrated in his new paper, "Feeling the Future: Experimental Evidence for Anomalous Retroactive Influences on Cognition and Affect," which was just published in "The Journal of Personality and Social Psychology". He had carried out experiments that gave positive indications that the phenomenon of Precognition is real-the details are summarized by

Jonah Lehrer in the paper "Feeling the future-is precognition real":

“Bem provided the following instructions to subjects before commencing the experiment:

> "This is an experiment that tests for ESP. It takes about 20 minutes and is run completely by computer. First, you will answer a couple of brief questions. Then, on each trial of the experiment, pictures of two curtains will appear on the screen side by side. One of them has a picture behind it; the other has a blank wall behind it. Your task is to click on the curtain that you feel has the picture behind it. The curtain will then open, permitting you to see if you selected the correct curtain. There will be 36 trials in all. Several of the pictures contain explicit erotic images (e.g., couples engaged in nonviolent but explicit consensual sexual acts). If you object to seeing such images, you should not participate in this experiment.

The location of the image was selected at random by the computer, which means that students should have correctly guessed the location of the pornography 50 percent of the time. However, it turned out that over 100 sessions, the subjects consistently performed above chance, and correctly located the porn 53.1 percent of the time.”

The various research results and the U.S. stargate project posit a strong view that the precognition ability does exist. The sporadic and spontaneous precognitive events are all before us to speak loudly that the incidents are real and not figs of imagination.

But still, there is an equal contrary view put forth by learned skeptics and there are enormous stumbling blocks in the way of Precognition being accepted as a scientific phenomenon.

The fact that mainstream science does not accept Parapsychology (inclusive of Precognition) as an established scientific field has been brought out in the introductory chapter of the book and several reasons which go against the subject being accepted as science have been discussed in details-all those reasons are applicable for precognition and those reasons go forward to support the views of skeptics. The reasons as above against Precognition gain more support through additional facts which makes precognition deviate from scientific principles:

*"Precognition violates the principle of antecedence (*causality*), that an effect does not happen before its cause.*

Information passing backward in time would need to be carried by physical particles doing the same. Experimental evidence from high-energy physics suggests that this cannot happen. There is therefore no direct justification for precognition from physics.

Precognition contradicts "most of the neuroscience and psychology literature, from electrophysiology and neuroimaging to temporal effects found in psychophysical research." It is considered a delusion *by mainstream* psychiatry.

The relatively new discovery of evidence for quantum retrocausality *is sometimes suggested as a possible mechanism for precognition. However, it is generally held that such "quantum weirdness", even if it is shown to exist, cannot carry information at a macroscopic level."* (source: *en.wikipedia.org/wiki/Precognition*)

Schwarzkopf (2014) illustrates his position against Precognition by citing his views that "… the future events influencing the past breaks the second law of thermodynamics… It also completely undermines over a century of experimental research based on the assumption that causes precede effects"

Precognition is not a scientific phenomenon as it stands now.

Skeptics have their own views against Precognition.

R.Wiseman (2011) dismisses precognition incidents as mere coincidences. He explains how precognitive dreams can be explained by the science of sleep--- he maintains that dream come true events are mere coincidences. We dream almost daily but tend to forget the same next day, but, even one dream, when resembles, even faintly, with the actually happened incident, it becomes a landmark.

There is an outburst from skeptics over the findings of Daryl Bem that his experimental results are statistically significant to prove that precognition exists. The article by Alan Boyle, Science Editor, NBC News (2011) carries the skeptics' views on the above findings of Daryl Bem. The article carries a statement from Ray Hyman, emeritus professor of psychology from the University of Oregon that the paper by Bem is nothing but craziness-pure craziness. "I can't believe a major journal is allowing this work in," Hyman

was quoted as saying. "I think it's just an embarrassment for the entire field."

Eric-Jan Wagenmakers, a psychologist at the University of Amsterdam, told the Times that Bem's research "should undergo more scrutiny before it is allowed to enter the field." Wagenmakers is a co-author of a rebuttal to the paper which is due to appear in the same issue of the journal.

The critics cite the same rule of skepticism promulgated by the late astronomer Carl Sagan: "Extraordinary claims require extraordinary evidence." These folks say Bem's experiments may have yielded seeming evidence of psychic phenomena or psi for short, but it's not extraordinary enough to meet the bar. They say it's just not statistically significant enough to allow for the conclusion that psychic powers exist. What's more, other scientists have had a hard time replicating Bem's results, as Scientific American's Michael Shermer noted in 2003.

Criticism against Precognition is substantiated by some research work on dream precognition

C. Watt, L. Vuillaume & R. Wiseman (2015) posit the following views in a paper written in the *Journal of Consciousness Studies:* "Controlled research into alleged psychic functioning can aid our understanding of the nature and limits of consciousness. Some commentators have suggested that the decline in positive results from dream precognition studies might be due to the early experiments being carried out in sleep laboratories whilst later studies tested participants in their own homes. The present study assessed this argument. Twenty participants were selected for prior precognitive dream experience, and were invited to a sleep laboratory. Participants were asked to dream about a target video they would later view. A judge rated participants' dreams against the target and decoys. No evidence was found for dream precognition. The study also tested the hypothesis that precognitive dream experiences may occur when a person subconsciously incorporates sensory information into their dream. A sound clip was played to sleeping participants and a judge rated the target and decoy clips against the participants' dream transcripts. The correlation between the degree of sensory incorporation and prior precognitive dream experience was non-significant."

The lobby of skeptics holds a strong view against precognition.

Thus, there are strong cases for and against the precognition phenomenon and we can’t conclusively say whether the phenomenon can have some scientific explanation. Even the study done jointly by researchers in favour of precognition together with those opposing it has not yielded a conclusive result – "*A proponent of evidence for psychic ability, and the second, a skeptic, have been conducting a systematic program of a collaborative skepticskeptic–proponent research in parapsychology. This has involved carrying out joint experiments in which each investigator individually attempted to mentally influence the electrodermal activity of participants at a distant location. The first two collaborations obtained evidence of 'experimenter effects, that is, experiments conducted by the proponent obtained significant results but those conducted by the skeptic did not. (Marilyn Schlitz, Richard Wiseman, Caroline Watt and Dean Radin, 2006)*

The research work by opponents to Precognition and the scientific facts opposing phenomenon are enormous but equally credible is the manifestation of sporadic and spontaneous precognitive incidents and the research conducted scientifically go on to prove that the results are statistically significant in favour of precognition phenomenon.

Thus, we come to an impasse about what to say about the phenomenon and as I mentioned in other aspects of the parapsychological field, the answer lies only in causal research on Precognition. While causal research has not happened for other parapsychological aspects there is research done by May and Marwaha which takes up the causal Precognition research.

The research paper by Sonali Marwaha and Edwin C May (2015) -- "***Rethinking Extrasensory Perception: towards a Multiphasic Model of Precognition***", does take a step towards causal research on Precognition. In this paper, the authors define precognition as an atypical perceptual ability that allows the acquisition of non-inferential information arising from a future point in space-time. Their Multiphasic Model of Precognition (MMPC) is summarized below:

"Precognition examines how we experience an event from a future spacetime point. It is very difficult to visualize how, when, where this information transfer occurs from a distant point in spacetime? Furthermore, what is the information carrier, and what are its properties? Answers to these questions will help to determine in which sensory system if any, the carrier energy is being converted into electrochemical signals. What is the transmission rate (bits/symbol) of the data, and what is its limit? At what point does the information occur: Is it at the source, transmission, or at the detection point? Further questions are who possesses

Precognition ability and why? Why can we not train fordeveloping a Precognition ability? Why do we not see a stable central nervous system (CNS) correlates with this ability?

To answer these questions, the authors approach the problem through two domains—Physics Domain (PD) and Neuroscience Domain (ND)

The physics domain (PD) tries to research how the information travels from distant future time points to present times. The theory of entropy (a measure of chaos) is used to help us understand the information flow.

Authors quote some experiments which show that the quality of Precognition is significantly correlated with changes of entropy of the target systems (May & Lantz, 2010/2014; May & Spottiswoode, 1994/2014; May et al., 2000), they propose that some aspect of entropy or its gradients will yield an understanding of the PD.

Entropy is a measure of chaos or the related idea of uncertainty. Ice, for example, has much lower entropy than water. Why? Because the molecules of water in liquid form are bouncing around chaotically, whereas in ice, these same molecules are all lined in an ordered array we call a crystal.

Shannon Entropy - Building on the pioneering work of Shannon and Weaver (1949) a theory was developed that is now called the information theory. This concept formalizes the intuitive idea of the information that there is more "information" in rare events, such as winning the lottery, than in common ones, such as taking a breath. Shannon and Weaver defined the entropy for a given system as the weighted average of the probability of occurrence of all possible events in the system. Entropy, used in this sense, is defined as a measure of our uncertainty, or lack of information, about a system.

The authors go on to say that it is possible to obtain information from some non-inferential event in the future. This, of course, violates the rules of macroscopic causality and the profound understanding that time moves in one direction only. Yet, at the microscopic level (i.e., atoms, molecules), the equations of motion are all symmetric in time. In other words, time could move forward or backward, and the collisions of molecules stay the same.

Many laboratory experiments reveal that the known sensory systems appear to be sensitive to entropic changes at their sensory "front ends,". Authors feel that it is not a surprise to find Precognition, too, is sensitive to entropic changes of the stimuli. They quote a theoretical article to explain how the Physics domain can make us understand Precognition.

The article by Verlinde (2011) developed the idea of an entropic force. This entropic force is like all other forces in that it is a spatial gradient of some potential. In addition, Verlinde was able to derive, again from first principles and gradients of entropy, the Einstein field equations of general relativity. The important point here is the supremacy of entropy as a physical concept. In fact, Verlinde goes so far as to suggest that it is time to retire gravity as one of the four known fundamental forces in that he shows that gravity itself is an emergent property of the more fundamental aspects of entropy and thermodynamics. Verlinde's work has spawned great interest in the fundamental nature of entropy.

Authors give their final considerations for the physics domain for explaining Precognition as follows:

"It is noted that there is considerable experimental evidence that suggests entropic gradients may be important in understanding the PD; ***however, with regard to mechanisms, signal carriers, and transducers, the evidence is circumstantial. Clearly, more work is needed."***

The Physics domain does not explain the understanding of information flow fully because it is stuck up to explain the mechanisms and working of signal carriers and transducers for which further research should be undertaken. However, the Physics Domain does open door to further causal Precognition research and the physicists must strive to find answers to the above questions to bring clarity about information flow.

"Neuroscience Domain (ND)—this domain studies the neurological processes that occur once the signals from any external source have reached the percipient's Central Neuro-system CNS, and the processes that occur from perception to cognition. This phase has three stages

- *Stage 1—the perception of precognition signals from an energy carrier,*
- *Stage 2—cortical processing of signals, and*
- *Stage 3- Cognition*

In precognition, stages 1 and 2 are critically different from normal perception in PC, following which, in Stage 3, normal processing occurs as it does for any other sensory input.

Stage 1- *In visual perception, the retina serves as a transducer as an interface between the incoming visual signal and the processor of the signal. On similar lines, the authors propose a special transducer in the case of perception of Precognition. Since the signals coming in*

Precognition, as seen, in the Physics domain are yet to be understood, this transducer which will depend on the signals is also to be researched after we succeed in research in the Physical domain.

As we know that the ability of precognition is not universal in all people, surveys have indicated that hardly 1% of the population has this ability.

Authors theorize that these people have s special transducer, details of which are matters of further research.

The final processing of the Precognition signals thus obtained occurs in the brain. This leads us to Stage 2 of the ND.

***Stage 2-** Cortical processing of Retro-Causal signals involves the processing of precognition signals received as stated in Stage 1.*

As there is variation in the incoming signal from the known perceptive signals, authors theorize their processing in a different mode -they call it processing via a cross-modal mechanism leading to a PC experience. They consider this notion by formulating the hypothesis of cortical hyper-associative mechanism.

Literature shows that Cortical hyper-connectivity has recently been associated with atypical perceptual abilities such as synaesthesia. Hence, they borrow the term hyper-associative mechanism for describing the possible underlying mechanisms.

Considering the possibility of similarity in underlying mechanisms between Synaesthesia and the proposed internal PC mechanism, in their view, the synesthete population may be a good point to start for examining this hypothesis. However, a crucial distinction between synaesthesia and PC experiences is that in Precognition the signals are external and not known as on date.

In synaesthesia, individual variations in cortical structure and functioning give rise to atypical cognition. They arise from a complex mix of genetic, sensory, and cortical architecture, and personal experiences that go into making each individual experience unique. Similarly, the Precognition ability may also be one such atypical experience. The authors hypothesize that cortical hyper-associative mechanisms may permit the processing of information acquired from a synaesthesia-like coupling to an extended sensory variability through a currently unknown transducer, following which the implicitly acquired data are further processed in the brain. Thus, there may be variability at the point of sensory signal intake.

In summary of Stages 1 and 2, RC signals may be acquired by an individual with Precognition ability, due to psychophysical variability in the signal transducer; these signals are then processed under Stage 2. The cortical hyper-associative mechanism takes advantage of a possible increase in the spectral range of EM and/or the perception of the precognitive signals that the brain can process.

Stage 3(Cognition)*—The authors hypothesize that in Stage 3, cognition occurs in the same manner as for other sensory inputs. The influence of emotions, memory, thinking, decision making, and so on occurs as it does for other non-Precognitive activity for eliciting a Precognitive response. In Stage 3, there is no distinguishing characteristic that differentiates the cognition of Precognition signals from that of normal sensory signals.*

The theory needs further research to overcome the challenges posed by the theory. They go on to dwell on these challenges as follows:

Authors see the primary challenges in the Physics Domain. Physicists are considering the possibility that the thermodynamic-derived single direction of time's arrow might be reversed on local or global scales. The main challenge is determining the nature of the precognitive signal carrier that propagates backward in time. The Retro-causal signal transducer depends on the carrier that can convert the energy from the carrier into a form that can be processed by the Central Nervous System. The nature of the transducer can provide clues to its location, just as the auditory receptors serve as a signal transducer for audio signals that can be subsequently

processed by the central auditory system. Identifying the transducer in PC ability may aid in exploring the physics domain for appropriate carriers and vice versa.

The challenges in the ND are not as onerous as in the PD. Having bifurcated the problem space, ND experimenters need not concern themselves with the challenges posed in the PD. As outlined, the primary problem for the ND is determining the nature of a Retro-Causal signal transducer and its cortical connectivity. This, in itself, will lead to a breakthrough in our understanding of the PD as well as the ND.

The basic process outlined in the MMPC opens the door for exploratory research, particularly for Stages 1 and 2 of the ND, which require expertise from a host of specialties. It is our sincere hope that experts from relevant disciplines take up the challenges posed, and take PC research forward.

As per the authors, the future challenges faced in their model is to find answers to: -

- What is the nature of retro-causal signal carrier that propagates backward movement in time (in Physics Domain)
- What is the nature of the Retro-causal signal transducer and its cortical connectivity (in the Neuroscience domain)?

The MMPC model provides a framework for future research to study fundamental questions regarding the nature of time, causality, and information.

Further research for PC (precognition) has to be in Physics Domain to find details of the retro-causal signal carrier that propagates backward movement in time.

Simultaneously work has to continue in the Neuroscience domain to find more details about the perception of retro-causal signal transducers and their cortical connectivity in the brain.

It is clearly evident that unless these unknown areas in physics and neuroscience are researched, we shall not be able to find answers to challenges posed in the neuroscience domain of the MMPC model.

The above paper, as per me, is a game-changer in the Causal research on Precognition and future researchers must take the research forward to put it on a firm footing by finding answers to the questions raised by the MMPC model.

I hope researchers from the science streams of Physics and Neuroscience jointly with Parapsychological Researchers will take research forward to bring it to a meaningful conclusion to unravel the crucial causal aspects concerning Precognition and then and only then the skeptics will cease to raise voice against precognition and we shall be able to stake our claim for it to be recognized as a stream of science.

In the next chapter, we take up Psychokinesis for discussions.

Chapter 5

Psychokinesis- on a rational pedestal

> *In the 1930s. A young gambler arrived at the Duke University parapsychology lab -- the first university lab fully dedicated to parapsychological research -- claiming he could influence the fall of dice by sheer «willpower». J.B.Rhine, director of the lab and 'father' of modern parapsychology, was intrigued, and ready and willing. He devised tests using dice as 'target' systems and found that the gambler indeed seemed to beat the odds and get the wished-for outcome much more often than would be expected by chance. Micro-Psychokinesis research was, thus, born, as the Rhine began to test different individuals' ability to influence the fall of dice.*
>
> (Mario Varvoglis, 2020)

In previous chapters we saw, Telepathy means mind to mind connection; Clairvoyance means seeing through the mind's eye and Precognition means mind looking at the future. Same way Psychokinesis means mind influencing matter.

In telepathy, we had discussed the 'Staring event' wherein the person is able to know that someone is staring without looking at the person. This clearly was a mind-to-mind connection i.e., Telepathy. But there is much more to it; the staring act does make the person being stared at uncomfortable, especially if the person being stared at is a female and the person staring is a male. Could this act of becoming uncomfortable not be due to mind-influencing a person i.e., Psychokinesis, in which not only mind to mind connection is made but mind gets influenced and body of the person being stared reacts to the gaze. We know that when sunrays are converged on a piece of carbon paper through a lens, so much heat generates that it burns the carbon paper. Maybe that the feeble energy generated by the act of staring is converging in the same fashion to create uneasiness to the person being stared at. Thus, the act of staring may be the mind's influence over the body of the person being stared at.

We have Psychokinesis instances from pre-historic times. In the Indian religious epic "Mahabharata, there is mention of gambling through the throw of dice between Kauravas led by prince Duryodhana and Pandavas led by prince Yudhistra. Kaurava's side had uncle Shakuni who possessed the Psychokinetic capability of mentally influencing the result of the dice throw. Using this psychokinetic ability Kauravas could win all possessions of Pandavas in the gambling game of dice throw.

Apart from Shakuni of Mahabharata, even Jesus is found using Psychokinesis to turn water into wine, heal the sick, and change a little bit of food into a lot as stated in Bible.

In recent times, the feats of URI Geller's spoon bending through gazing over it are etched in history as the manifestation of Psychokinesis. Geller was born on 20 December 1946 in Tel Aviv, which was then part of British-administered Mandatory Palestine. His mother and father were of Austrian-Jewish and Hungarian-Jewish backgrounds respectively. At the age of 11, Geller's family moved to Nicosia, Cyprus, where he attended high school, the Terra Santa College, and learned English.

Geller first started to perform in theatres, public halls, auditoriums, military bases, and universities in Israel. By the 1970s, Geller had become known in the United States and Europe. He also received attention from the scientific community, whose members were interested in examining his reported psychic abilities. His performance included spoon bending, describing hidden drawings, and making watches stop or run faster. Geller said he performs these feats through willpower and the strength of his mind.

The parapsychologist Andrija Puharich met Geller in 1971 and endorsed him as a genuine psychic.

Geller's spoon bending feats were discussed in *The Geller Papers* (1976), edited by Charles Panati. There was controversy when it was published. Several prominent magicians came forward to demonstrate that Geller's psychic feats could be duplicated by stage magic. James Randi has also shown that Geller's tricks can be replicated with stage magic techniques. (Wikipedia *ttps://en.wikipedia.org/wiki/Uri_Geller*)

Geller admitted that though his feats could be done by magicians but maintained that he had been doing these through paranormal powers.

Geller lost credibility in face of skeptics' view and his own admission as above.

Uri Geller was a famous personality doing psychokinetic feats, equally famous are the feats that were done by ***Nina Kulagina***.

Nina Kulagina was born on July 30, 1926, in Leningrad. She was very much an average, tough Russian woman possessing psychic powers including the psychokinetic ability. Nina claimed that she was always aware of her 'psychic powers'. There are stories that she could mentally see things inside people's pockets, and when she met sick people, she could identify the disease they were suffering from, an image of the illness appearing in her mind. On one occasion when Kulagina was in a particularly angry mood, she was walking towards a cupboard in her apartment when a jug in the cupboard suddenly moved to the edge of the shelf, fell, and smashed to pieces on the floor. After that changes began to take place in her apartment. Lights went on and off; objects became animated and seemed somehow to be attracted to her. It was in effect a type of poltergeist activity, except that Kulagina was convinced the psychic power was coming from her and discovered that, if she tried, she could control it.

One of Kulagina's abilities involved her sitting at a table and staring at a small object, such as a matchbox or a wineglass, and make it move without touching it. Apparently, her powers did not come straight away, hours of preparation may be needed, which, as skeptics have pointed out, does not favour the setting up of strictly supervised demonstrations. In order to move things with mind power alone, she found she had to clear all other thoughts from her head and told investigators that when her concentration was successful, there was a sharp pain in her spine, and her eyesight blurred. Nina practiced hard, focusing her powers, and was soon able to move matchsticks, fountain pens, and compass needles. There is nothing here, however, which an accomplished stage magician could not duplicate, though no one at the time in Russia seems to have bothered to try. (source: *mysteriouspeople.com/Nina_Kulagina.htm*)

One of the first scientists to take an interest in Kulagina was Biologist Edward Naumov. In an early test, the details of which are as usual sketchy, he scattered a box of matches on a bench; Nina held her hands over them, trembling with the strain. Suddenly, all the matches moved together to the edge of the bench, then fell one by one to the floor.

Amazing stories about Nina Kulagina began to reach the West through the international wire services in the spring of 1968. In the same year, films of Kulagina moving objects, ostensibly using only her mind, were shown at the First Moscow International Conference on Parapsychology and were also seen by some Western scientists.

Like Uri Geller she also came under scrutiny of sceptics and non-believers in psychic phenomena. A paper titled The psychic powers of Nina Kulagina are just too crazy!-Strange Sounds (Feb 24, 2016) gives an account of skeptics' views on her capability:

"*With the scientific community catching wind of Nina's astounding feats came to the heavy hand of scrutiny. Skeptics including James Randi have long maintained that none of Nina's apparent psychic abilities was anything more than common trickery and sleight of hand illusions. Just like Uri Gellar, Nina's publicized experiments were never under ideal laboratory conditions. She was seen at home or in hotel rooms, without experts in trickery on hand. It's been claimed that Nina had magnets implanted into her body to manipulate objects; other telekinetic claims could have employed the use of thin wires or mirrors. Yet in the USSR, laboratory experiments were performed on Nina (under the pseudonym Nelya Mikhailova) by several researchers, including Czech psychical researcher Dr. Zdenek Rejdak, psychologist B. Blazek, physicist V. F. Shvetz, Dr. J.S. Zvierev, physiologist L.L. Vasiliev, and the aforementioned Dr. Sergeyev. Dr. Rejdak published a report of his experiments (titled 'Nina Kulagina's Mind over Matter') in the June 1971 issue of Psychic Magazine.*

It has been argued that Nina was shown off by the USSR in an effort to make it seem like they were making huge leaps in telekinesis when in fact it was all fakery. But even though the Cold War has long since ended, Russia has continued to keep many of its secrets under lock and key. If Nina was such a glowing success, where are the scientific reports? Might they still be housed somewhere in a storage room never to see the light of day? As is the case with so many things, just because we haven't seen something doesn't mean it doesn't exist.

Near the end of her life, Nina seems to have lost the abilities she became so famous for. Her exertion in manifesting these powers was blamed for a near-fatal heart attack in the late 1970s. Sharp pain in her spine, dizziness, blood sugar irregularities, failing eyesight, and many other health concerns plagued her. With deteriorating health, Nina stepped away from the endless scientific testing, conducting very limited experiments in labs up until her death in 1990. And so, the full truth died with her. Whether or not she ever possessed remarkable abilities, perhaps faking it when her powers disappeared later in life, is a matter of speculation."

The above two are very prominent large-scale or macro-psychokinesis events for which we saw both proponent and opponent views.

One similar famous macro-PK event is of ***Katie, the Gold Leaf Lady***

Katie, the Gold Leaf Lady was an illiterate housewife in Florida USA who claimed that a gold-colored foil would appear spontaneously on her skin during her everyday life and it was unexplainable. Parapsychologist Stephan Braude, in one of the sessions with her in 1997 managed to film foil seemingly emerging out on Katie's face, after she rubbed her eye a few times with her finger. Several other researchers observed this phenomenon of golden foil emerging on her abdomen or other parts of the body. Several researchers and also magician Christopher Chacon had investigated this phenomenon and had thoroughly frisked her for any extra material hidden around her body before they commenced their sessions and they could not find any clue behind the manifestation of this phenomenon. The mystery of Katie remains unresolved to date (Watt Caroline 2016).

Another famous macro-PK incident regarding a Chicago elevator ***Ted Serios*** finds mention in Caroline's book, who was found to paranormally cause images to appear on photographic film. Serios will hold a small black tube to his forehead (which he said helped him to focus his thought waves), then he would place the tube in front of the lens of a Polaroid camera. Some photographs were found to show distinct shapes or slightly blurred images of buildings and graphical locations. His miraculous feat was examined by psychiatrist Jule Esienbud from university of Colorada and after close scrutiny and study Eisenbud, eventually, became convinced that Serios, indeed, possessed genuine paranormal powers.

Later this was claimed by a skilled magician and Harvard Statistician Persi Diaconis that such a feat was possible through several ways; for instance, by inserting a small image into the tube. But this claim was criticized by many including Braude that sleight of hand for inserting anything in the tube was ruled out because Serios had no physical contact with the camera. This feat could not be replicated by skeptics and the mystery behind this also stands unresolved to date.

Looking to the credible macro-PK phenomena, some of which were proven fraudulent and for others, no clues are yet found, Caroline Watt (2016) made important observations: *Over the years*, many people have claimed to possess macro-PK abilities but investigations have brought out that some of them were frauds, However, there exists some for which an explanation could not be found out. But the skeptics believe that such feats were not carried out under most controlled conditions. The overall majority of parapsychologists do not find the evidence compelling in favour of macro-PK or large-scale psychokinesis.

Having discussed some large-scale Psychokinetic incidences, and prominent people presumably possessing psychokinetic ability, we shall, now, take a short journey into the history of Psychokinesis Research which will also cover micro-PK i.e., experimental laboratory psychokinesis research:

A brief history of Research on Psychokinesis (PK)

As per Mario Varvoglis (2020) and Raga Sukma(2009), Psychokinesis, a form of psi, meaning that, apparently, it is a technique of mind influencing matter through invisible means.

Examples of PK are movements of objects, bending of metals, and influencing the outcome of events. It can occur spontaneously and deliberately.

The study of phenomena said to be Psychokinesis is an aspect of Parapsychology. Some paranormal researchers believe that psychokinesis exists and deserves further study, although the focus of research has shifted away from large-scale phenomena *Macroscopic' or large-scale PK effects* to *Microscopic* e.g., attempts to influence dice and then to random number generators.

Raga Sukma (2009) posits in his paper that "The term psychokinesis is derived from the Greek words psyche meaning "breath," "life," or "soul," and kinesin meaning "to move." The occurrences of PK have been recorded since ancient times. The occurrences include levitation, miraculous healings, luminosities, apports, and other physical phenomena attributed to holy persons and adepts of magic around the world. Such phenomena are recorded in the Bible, especially in the New Testament, in the Book of Acts. One example is cited in which St. Paul and Silas were imprisoned in Ephesus where they prayed and sang hymns, and at midnight their shackles fell off as the prison doors swung opened (Acts 16:19-40).

It is thought that possibly magic spells, curses, and rituals to control the weather may involve PK. The use of the evil eye has been placed within this classification.

Manifestations of PK have occurred in spiritualism such as alleged materializations and dematerializations, apports, levitations, table-tipping, raps, and the appearances of ectoplasm and pseudopods.

Mario Varvoglis (2020) mentions that-Actually, the idea of micro-PK is not new. Way back in the 1700s, Sir Francis Bacon, 'father' of the scientific method, gave some visionary suggestions for the study of micro-

PK. In his posthumously published work « Sylva Sylvarum » he proposed we study this 'mental force' by applying it «...upon things that have the lightest and easiest motions... as upon the sudden fading or coming up of herbs; or upon their bending one way or other ...or upon the casting of dice».

Raga Sukma(2009) talks about Psychokinesis manifestations from the nineteenth century onwards: During the 19th century, D. D. Holmes was known for his ability to levitate and to handle hot coals without being burned. But, also during this time, there were individuals known as "electric people" who experienced a "high-voltage syndrome". They made knives and forks cling to their skin, and with touch could send furniture flying across a room.

At the beginning of the 20th century Rudi Schneider, another medium known for his PK ability of materialization and telekinesis of objects, was studied by psychical researchers.

Twentieth-century research:

Since the 1930s interest in PK has increased until it has created one of the fastest-growing fields of research in parapsychology. This is particularly true within the Soviet Union and the United States.

However, results from clinical-controlled studies have been contradictory. Some of the studies were attacked for the methodology while others were accused of being tainted by fraud.

It can be stated that psychokinesis does occur, by the necessary conditions and requirements for its occurrence. Patterns have been identified according to experimenters and subjects, but it is known such patterns do not apply in all circumstances.

An American parapsychologist at Duke University in North Carolina, J. B. Rhine began conducting PK experiments in 1934. Although he was not the first to study PK, he did so after conducting ESP experiments which yielded significant results."

Following observation by Mario Varvoglis (2020) has this to add to the above narration.

"A young gambler arrived at the Duke University parapsychology lab -- the first university lab fully dedicated to parapsychological research -- claiming he could influence the fall of dice by sheer «willpower». J.B.Rhine, director of the lab and 'father' of modern parapsychology, was intrigued, and ready and willing. He devised tests using dice as 'target' systems, and found that the gambler indeed seemed to

beat the odds and get the wished-for outcome much more often than would be expected by chance. Micro-PK research was thus born, as Rhine began to test different individuals' ability to influence the fall of dice."

Continuing the narration Raga Sukma posits-

"Early experimental data showed results far beyond the probabilities of chance, but later testing data yielded uneven results. Rhine did not immediately publish his findings for several reasons: PK suffered a dubious reputation at the time; he had occasionally used himself as a subject, and his studies were very insignificantly controlled. He finally published his findings when an assistant noted that subjects scored significantly better at the dice in the early part of the sessions than toward the end. This tendency attributed to a decrease of interest on the part of the subjects had been observed in ESP experiments too.

In the publication of his experiments, Rhine reported that he observed that PK does not seem to connect with any physical process of the brain or to be subject to any of the mechanical laws of physics. Rather, it does seem to be a nonphysical force of the mind that can act on the matter in statically measurably ways. The results produced cannot be explained by physics."

The recent research is well laid out by Mario Varvoglis and Peter Bancel (2015) in their book Micro-Psychokinesis. Some excerpts from the book give details of recent research in the field:

The field changed quickly when researchers turned towards an entirely novel generation of PK target systems based on the intrinsically indeterminate processes associated with quantum phenomena, such as the decay of radioactive isotopes. Following several researchers' inconclusive attempts in this direction, the physicist Helmut Schmidt created a relatively compact and flexible device using a strontium-90 source. Schmidt's device used the detection of radioactive decay at a Geiger counter to stop and register the state of a high-frequency two-state counter. Since the decay occurs at random intervals, the counter is equally likely to stop in either state, and the output is thus equivalent to the toss of a fair coin. The quantum indeterminacy of the decay, guaranteeing the randomicity and independence of the successive outputs, can thus be readily used as the basis of a precognition task (guessing the outcome of the next 'coin toss'). It could also be used as a PK experiment by asking the subject to intend or wish for a particular outcome, then initiate a trial with a button-push and receive immediate feedback.

Micro-PK - The PEAR Research

The Princeton Engineering Anomalies Research (PEAR) laboratory was founded by Robert Jahn, Dean of the engineering school at Princeton. He assembled a staff of physicists, psychologists, and technicians who worked in a basement lab of the campus engineering building for nearly 30 years (the PEAR lab closed in 2007). PEAR's primary focus was micro-PK RNG research, although extensive effort also included work on macroscopic random systems (some reminiscent of the Rhine era), and remote viewing studies. Like Schmidt, PEAR built its own RNGs in-house Extensive testing and calibrations were published and there is little doubt that the devices were reliable and stable enough to detect the small effect sizes expected in the universalist approach.

RNG used a binary device that produced feedback as either a counter readout or a graphical display. Data were generated at the rate of one trial per second and consisted of the sum of 200 consecutive random 0 or 1 bits (the expected mean trial output thus being 100)10. All the RNGs in the PEAR lab used exclusive-OR (XOR) processing of the raw bits before summed to make a trial, to eliminate potential first-order biases in the bitstreams

PEAR used a 'tripolar' protocol for each experimental run, which consisted of three separate PK efforts of equal length. These were termed HI, LO, and BL (baseline) and indicated the direction of the participants' intention: bias the output to go high, to go low, or to remain even. The experimental hypothesis was then that the HI runs would give a positive deviation from the mean and the LO runs a negative deviation. The statistical test was based on the difference between the two directional runs. The BL run was intended as a control and the participants' instructions were to hold no intention while the baseline data accumulated.

A particularity of the lab was to conduct long-term studies of a single protocol over many years.

Rather than designing short studies with a pre-set number of trials, major experiments were cumulative, and occasional updates of progress would be communicated in reports or publications. While not all work followed this open-ended model, the most important and consequential micro-PK experiment did (Jahn et al., 1997). This was the so-called 'benchmark' experiment, a twelve-year study that collected over 2.5 million experimental trials from 91 participants. At its termination, the experiment had attained a high significance, yielding a Z-score of 3.8."

The research work on Psychokinesis has been to establish proof that there exists a capability in the human mind to influence the matter without using any external means. On one side there were attempts to prove that the phenomenon is real, on the other side, as is usual for bizarre phenomena, there were skeptics who were airing their views that the psychokinetic feats were due to frauds/trickery and magic.

Skeptics' views against Psychokinesis

The skeptics state that the Psychokinesis feats (including the spoon bending act) are nothing but trickery—Terence Hines a science writer quotes Harris Ben (1985) that Geller has been caught many times using sleight of hand and all his effects have been recreated using conjuring tricks. Among many skeptics, James Randi has also shown that Geller's tricks can be replicated with stage magic techniques.

Wiseman R (2011) in his book, "Paranormality, why we see what isn't there" suggests that feats like spoon bending can be easily performed by doing some advanced preparation and hence these are mere trickery.

In fact, we cannot blame only skeptics for dismissing the idea of psychokinesis out of hand. The theory definitely has a few things working against it:

High Probability of Fraud. –The so-called paranormal feats of psychokinesis could also be performed through magic tricks.

It will be interesting to see how magic can manifest psychokinetic feats; The following are simple examples of magic tricks that present the feats which otherwise could be misunderstood as the result of the psychokinetic ability of the person (source: *mindblowingmagic.com/how-to-telekinesis/*):

Psychokinetic Straw & Bottle-- A Magical trick

You can use any bottle. I prefer the type with a cap that isn't completely flat, like the one seen in the picture. Since the straw isn't fully balanced it will move more. Rip off an inch or two on one end of the straw wrapper. Grip the wrapper at the rip and slide it all the way down and off the straw. This will charge the straw with static electricity. Balance the straw on top of the cap. Bring your fingers close to the charged end of the straw. Static electricity will cause the straw to move toward your fingers. It is pretty

cool to play with. To make this trick look good, like real telekinesis, hold your fingers above and your thumb near the end of the straw.

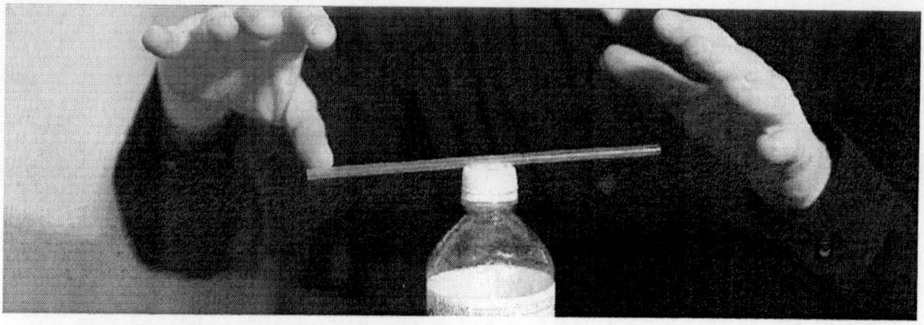

Your thumb will attract and move the straw. Wiggle your 1st finger at the same time so it looks like you are moving the straw from above. ***Slowly*** bring your thumb close to the charged end. When the straw moves gently move your thumb up and away. The straw will spin on the cap. When it slows down bring your hand close to the straw again to give it more momentum.

Once you take the straw off the bottle and put it down it will lose its charge and your spectator can try.

Performance Tips: Do it only one- or two times max.

Don't call attention to the straw when you remove the wrapper. You don't need to squeeze that hard, a little charge goes a long way.

Be gentle when balancing the straw so it doesn't fall. Play with it a bunch of times so you can balance it consistently.

If the straw falls while balancing it might lose its charge. You can try picking it up and proceeding. If it did lose its charge move on to another trick. After that open another straw and retry.

Straw is very light and doesn't need that much charge. If you find the straw is clinging to you like a magnet, charge it less.

No Wrapper**:** Another way to static charge the straw is to wrap your shirt around it and rub it a few times. The best time to do this is before the trick starts when nobody is looking. Turn away and charge it quickly. Takes 2 seconds.

Another magical trick can be done using PEN & BOTTLE:

TELEKINETIC PEN

You can use any bottle. I prefer the type with a cap that isn't completely flat, like the one seen in the picture. Since the pen isn't fully balanced it will move more.

A basic round pen is best. The trick is the same as the telekinetic straw. You will need to static charge the pen. Wrap your shirt around the pen and rub it a few times. The best time to do this is before the trick starts when nobody is looking. Turn away and charge it quickly. Takes 2 seconds.

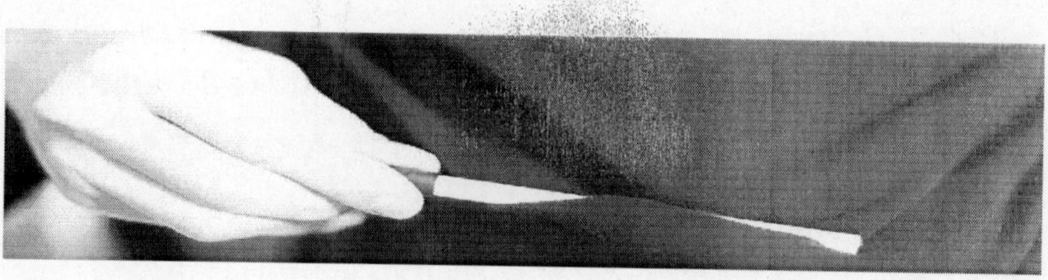

Pen Charging

Balance the pen on top of the cap. Hold your fingers above and your thumb near the end of the pen. Your thumb will attract and move the pen. Wiggle your 1st finger at the same time so it looks like you are moving the pen from above. ***Slowly*** bring your thumb near the charged end. When the pen moves gently move your thumb up and away. The pen will spin. When it slows down bring your hand close to the pen to give it more momentum.

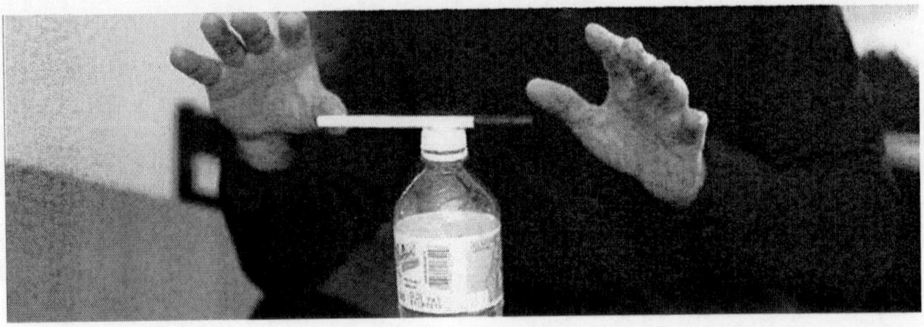

Once you take the pen off the bottle and put it down it will lose its charge and your spectator may try.

If the pen falls while balancing it might lose its charge. You can try picking it up and proceeding. If it did lose its charge move on to another trick. Recharge the pen at the right moment.

PRO TIP: Practice balancing the pen a few times before you do the trick so you know the right spot. You don't want to drop the charged pen in the middle of the performance.

Telekinetic Post-It Note—another magical trick

This is an amazing trick you are going to love. It is so cool. It will seem as if you just point your finger at the paper and it falls over. Take any post-it note or small piece of paper. Fold it slightly so it can balance on its edge. Place it on the table in front of you. Rub your hands together in front of your body as if getting energy.

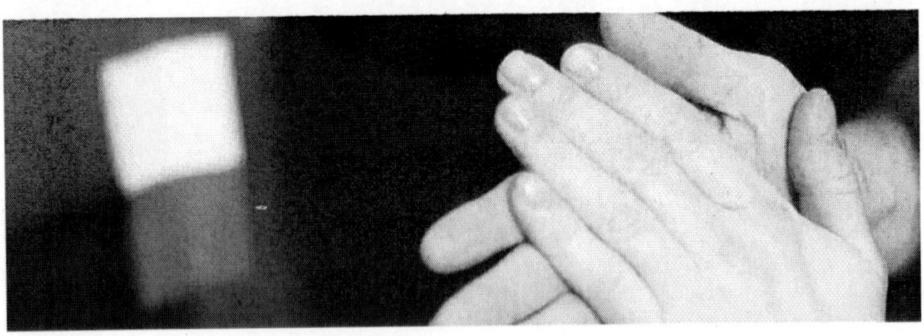

Move your hand forward and point at the paper. Bring your finger to about an inch away. Nothing will happen. Do these two more times. On the 3rd time briskly move your ***flat*** hand toward the paper and point your finger. Your quick movement will create an air current that is slightly behind your hand. A split second later the air will catch up and knock over the paper.

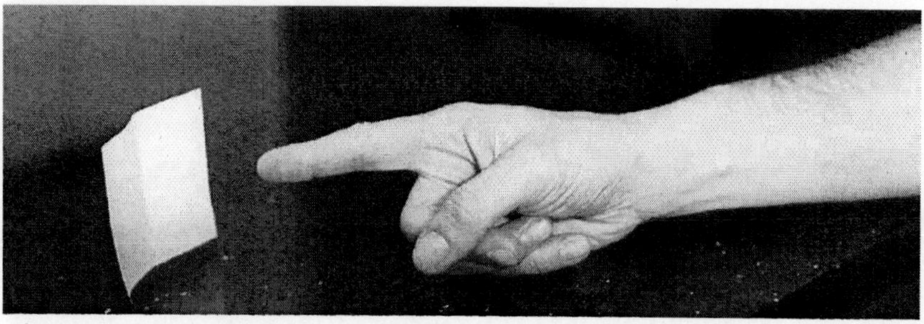

Since the air current comes after your finger is already extended, it looks like the energy in your finger knocked over the paper.

The above tricks will always hover over our minds when someone claiming to possess psychokinetic ability gives a demo of his/her capability. The tricks above are easy to perform but powerful enough to fool the audience.

Skeptics have looked for these subtle tricks in the staged psychokinetic performances and could sometimes succeed in proving the frauds.

The aspect of fraud/ trickery is a big hurdle for psychokinesis getting accepted as a scientific event. Even Uri Geller admitted that the spoon-bending act could also be performed by magicians who having done the same advanced preparation could bend the spoon by gazing at it. In fact, as discussed above Wiseman (2011) showed the way how it could be done with pre-planning.

Apart from the magical tricks, there is another factor which goes against the phenomenon of Psychokinesis viz., the psychokinesis research really isn't very compelling—even the micro-psychokinesis research involving dice throwing or random number generating experiments which have given statistically significant results, the significance was marginal.

Here, the words from astronomer Carl Sagan echoes in my mind—***"Extra-ordinary claims require Extra-ordinary Evidence".*** Skeptics hold the view that either the micro PK experiments had design flaws or the marginally statistically significant results obtained by beaming parapsychologists were certainly not the extra-ordinary proofs befitting the extraordinary psychokinetic phenomena.

There remains doubt among the scientific community on the existence of micro-PK given:

- the small and heterogeneous effect; and
- the fact that several independent replication attempts of prominent studies failed to confirm the original results.(Markus A. Maier, Moritz C. Dechamps *and Markus Pflitsch, 2018 of Department of Psychology, Ludwig-Maximilians-Universität München, Munich, Germany).* The details of the study can be referred in their paper using the hyperlink - *https://doi.org/10.3389/fpsyg.2018.00379.*

A paper by Bosch Holger, Fiona Steinkamp, and Emil Boller (2006) holds the view that even the marginal statistically significant results in Micro Psychokinesis experiments (of dice–throwing or Random number generators) do not go to prove that the results obtained were due to Psychokinesis.: *"Experimental research has reduced these phenomena to attempts to influence (a) the fall of dice and, later, (b) the output of random number generators (RNGs). The meta-analysis combined 380 studies that assessed whether RNG output correlated with human intention and found a significant but very small overall effect size. The study effect sizes were strongly and inversely related to sample size and were extremely heterogeneous. A Monte Carlo simulation revealed that the small effect size, the relation between sample size and effect size, and the extreme effect size heterogeneity found could in principle be a result of publication bias."*

While the above paper hints that even the small statistically significant results obtained could be due to reasons other than Psychokinesis, it would be relevant to discuss the role of statistical significance in experimental research as explained by Jessica Utts:

"Jessica Utts (1999) is of the view that it is the role of statistics to identify and quantify important effects and relationships before any explanation is found in research. Statistical methods are of use at the discovery phase of research. Only after such a study indicates a possibility that a relationship or effect exists, the justification stage of research starts where the use of that particular field of science attempts to find causal aspects of the effect."

In psi research, the statistical tool assumes a null hypothesis that the effect seen is not caused by chance only and the data collected is subjected to statistical tests of significance. In case when null hypothesis gets rejected strongly, the effect can be thought of due to some assignable cause. But finding out what those causes are is not within the scope of Statistics. The absence of chance causes does not necessarily mean that psi is the cause.

The research needs to be further pursued to find the real root-cause which is behind the phenomenon.

The above point is repeatedly brought forth by me – when there are strong views both for and against the Parapsychological phenomena, then, the answer lies only in the causal research -and this goes for the Psychokinesis as well.

In the next few paragraphs we shall see how we can trend towards Causal Psychokinesis Research:

Trending towards Causal Psychokinesis Research

The research so far has been concentrated to prove that phenomenon of Psychokinesis is real but how these happen, is a matter of *Causal Research.*

Can the mind emit energy to influence matter?

R Douglous Fields (2008) writes in Scientific American, "All our thoughts, sensations and actions arise from bioelectricity generated by neurons and transmitted through complex neural circuits inside our skull. Electrical signals between neurons generate electric fields that radiate out of brain tissue as electrical waves that can be picked up by electrodes touching a person's scalp. Measurements of such brainwaves in EEGs provide powerful insight into brain function"

Thus, the mind does produce energy waves that can be picked up by EEG. Are these energy waves so powerful that their use can affect external matter?

"The human brain does emit waves, like when a person focuses his attention or remembers something. This activity fires thousands of neurons simultaneously at the same frequency generating a wave—but at a rate closer to 10 to 100 cycles per second. *Beta waves (13-38 Hz) occur when we are actively thinking, problem-solving, etc.*

Researchers at MIT say that Brain waves are so weak, they are hardly measurable at all. The magnetic field of the earth is just strong enough to move the needle of a compass. Signals from the brain are a billionth of that strength." (*quora.com/What-kind-of-energy- waves-does-our-brain-emit-while-thinking-process*)

The above means that the energy waves emitted by the mind are very-very feeble and must not be capable of influencing the external matter.

However, we know that energy, when concentrated/ focused, gathers a lot of potentials to impact other matters. As was pointed out earlier also, we have seen that when we place a lens over a paper and let sun rays pass through the lens and then on to paper, the paper burns after some time. The rays carrying heat become focused and converge on a point on the paper and the intensity of heat rises to burn the paper.

Could there be a way that the waves from the mind could get powerfully converged on the matter in a way similar to converging light rays to a single pointand gain the power to influencing external matter, thus, resulting in the manifestation of Psychokinesis?

Though logical, the idea appears to be far-fetched to be true. Maybe, still, there is some way that such feeble waves got made robust, and resulted in the manifestation of Psychokinetic feats. Further research on how the energy waves reached the power to influence matter through its increased strength will form an approach towards understanding the causal aspects of Psychokinesis. This is purely in the domain of Physics and we hope that scientific research will uncover how the energy waves could gain immense strength to influence matter.

Also, I wish to reiterate here, that like other aspects of psi, Psychokinesis also involves the working of the mind, hence, a clue to causal research, certainly, lies in a higher understanding of the working of the mind. Only an advancement in Neuroscience will show us the way. Physicists and Neuroscientists must collaborate together to take Causal Psychokinesis Research forward.

The discussions in the above paragraphs have shown that the Micro-Psychokinesis- a form of Psychokinesis has been researched extensively compared to Macro-Psychokinesis and as observed above, many research papers have been written on Micro-PK. But causal research is yet to be taken up.

Mario Varvoglis and Peter Bancel (2015), in their paper Micro-Psychokinesis suggest that the most interesting question is the one for which we have the least to offer by way of an answer: how do we explain micro-PK? We are very far from being able to claim to understand micro-PK, and several competing (or complementary) models need to be systematically evaluated, such as retro-causal models, observational theories, and generalized quantum theory. We can only hope that more theory-driven research will emerge in near future and elucidate the nature of micro-PK.

Dean Radin (2006) in his book, "Entangled Minds" does talk about Quantum Theories relating to ESP/PK phenomena---He goes on to say that the theories of psi were inspired by Quantum Mechanics.

The following paragraphs give summaries of some of those theories which if pursued may lead us to causal research of Psychokinesis and other aspects of Parapsychological fields of study:

- ***Observational theory***—Retro PK experiment runs like this-Suppose random data-like a series of random bits, was automatically recorded on a computer hard disk without anyone observing them, then those recorded bits would remain in an indefinite state until they were observed. After being observed, they would collapse into actual bits.
  The predictions resulted in experiments in which the previously recorded, unobserved random bits were observed later according to instructions, "aim for 1s" or "aim for 0s. The results were consistent with the prediction that the act of observation retroactively influences quantum events. Thus, Observational theory became one of the first theories of psi to predict and successfully confirm an outrageous time-reversed effect. The theory proposed in the 1970s was motivated by similarities between the non-local properties of Quantum Wave function and the space-time independence of psi phenomena, and also by the quantum measurement problem, which offers the possibility that the mind plays an important role in physical reality. The theory resonates well with the thinking of noble laureate Eugene Winger that action of matter on the mind must give rise to direct action of mind upon the matter.

Numerous Researchers have come to a conclusion that the act of observing a quantum event probabilistically influences its outcome.

- ***Model of Pragmatic Information***—In this model physicist and psychologist Walter Von Lucadou proposes that the basic quantum theory might apply in a more general way to basic relationships between information, space, and time –the aspects deeply related to psi.

  His model assumes that structure and the function of a system are complementary; in fact, they are inextricably entangled. From this complementary relationship, according to him, an uncertain relationship that rests on "Pragmatic Information" can be derived. As with any uncertainty relationship, we can't measure both structure and function because these properties are entangled. If we try to measure function, then the means of measuring changes the structure Von Lucadou's model proposes that psi effects arise in non-local correlations that derive from the entangled structure-function relationship.

- ***Quantum Theory- Stapp-Von Neumann's approach***- This Hungarian mathematician placed the foundation of Quantum Theory on firm mathematical ground. His interpretation assumes that Quantum theory tells us about knowledge of "Reality" rather than "Reality itself and that the observing instrument and the observer are part of the whole system. He theorizes that since an observer and his/ her knowledge is a key component in the quantum measurement process, hence, the mind is inextricably entangled into quantum reality. As per him, this approach overcomes a limitation in how consciousness is understood within classical physics. From a classical physics point of view, the "You" who is reading these lines is an illusion. This is an important limitation because people believe that they (their conscious mind) do exist and are not an illusion.

  The Stapp Von Neumann approach solves this problem by putting the mind back into the Quantum-measurement process. It proceeds through two events—Process 1-involves the mind asking a question about Nature and Process 2 is the response. Process 1 probes Nature from 'Outside" the usual constraint of space and time (and is thus a nonlocal process), whereas Process 2 is what we observe within Nature, and thus limited by ordinary space-time- As per Stapp in classical Physics the elemental ingredients are tiny bits of matter that are idealized miniaturized versions of the planet that moves in a way unaffected by our scrutiny, whereas in quantum physics the elemental ingredients are intentional actions by agents (i.e., minds), the feedback arising from these actions, and the effects of our actions on the physical states that embody or carry this information.

The above suggests that the mind/brain might be a self-observing quantum object and as such, it resides within an entangled, non-local medium that just happens to be entirely compatible with the unknown characteristics of psi.

The way forward to Causal Psychokinesis is not laid out as clearly as was for Telepathy or Precognition but one thing is certain that the efforts of Physicists especially in the area of Quantum Physics will lead us to some clue.

Also, since Psychokinesis emanates from the mind and we know too little about the mind, it is logical to assume that if Neuroscientists research and uncoverthe mystery of the mind, we may find a way to explain how the mind influences matter.

The trend towards Causal research is very hazy and is not well laid out in the case of Psychokinesis and a lot of efforts on Psychokinesis Research is needed to find a way to causal research.

One thing, though, is sure- the confusion arising in mind due to proponent and opponent views on Psychokinesis will only get cleared by pursuing the Causal Psychokinesis Research.

We shall, now, take up the most difficult and the only aspect of Parapsychology which could be taken up for experimental research in laboratories—Life after Death.

Chapter 6

Life After Death- Does it exist

The appearance of apparitions has baffled many of us for ages and no explanation is found. The most bizarre are the instances concerning Abraham Lincoln who manifested as an apparition on several occasions which were witnessed by different eminent people at different times. There is a mention of these in the book by ***Judith Ennamorato*** *(2006): During one of his visits to the States during world war two, Winston Churchill spent the night at the white house. On one occasion, he climbed out of the bath and naked, save for the Cigar, sauntered into the adjoining bedroom. Startled, he looked up to see Abraham Lincoln standing by the fireplace in the room, leaning on the mantle. Churchill simply blinked before saying, "You seem to have me at a disadvantage,". Lincoln apparently smiled softly before simply disappearing.*

If at all there is one single universal truth-it is ***Death.*** All who are born are sure to die. But the word ***"Death"*** just shudders chill along our spine and we are so much scared of it that we simply do not want to talk about it. Each of us knows that death is certain but as for diseases, we think that it is for others and not for me. It cannot happen to me. When we go and attend the funeral of our loved ones, we become philosophical in the crematorium/graveyard because the environment pushes us into that frame of mind. We start thinking and wondering what happens when and after we die. Religious sermons detailing the philosophical explanation occupy our thoughts and we are emotionally moved. But soon after when we resume normal activities in our life, we forget that frame of mind, and the idea of death is brushed aside and forgotten.

Distancing ourselves from the thoughts of death makes us live in a fool's paradise. An apt analogy could be a pigeon closing its eyes to become sure that cat is not around. Shutting our thoughts from death does not make us immortal. The illusion created by the pigeon makes it easy prey to cat; likewise, we shall be surprised to face death when it stalks and reaches us. Whatever we do, we cannot avoid it.

While none of us want to talk about death but all of us are very curious to know what happens after death. We do not know how we feel when we are dying. The mystery shrouding death and what happens after we die is not resolved to date just because the person experiencing death does not come back to tell the experience. So, we are ignorant about these aspects for ages. Ignorance breeds fear and fear is what we experience when mention is made about death and the afterlife. We do not know about it so as is human nature we keep on imagining this mysterious unknown field. This universal truth makes us philosophical and the philosophical thoughts about death have been fascinating thinkers and philosophers from pre-historic times. They have been expressing their thoughts about death and after-life.

The Philosophy book (2011) makes mention of Pythagoras (c.570) who believed in reincarnation and the transmigration of souls... For him, the goal of life is freedom from the cycle of reincarnation, which can be gained by adhering to a strict set of behavioural rules.

The book, also, captures the thoughts of Buddha-Siddhartha Gautam (c.563-483BCE). In his era, the dominant faith in the Indian subcontinent was Brahmanism-a religion that had evolved from Vedism- an ancient belief based on the sacred Veda Texts. Siddhartha Gautam was the first to challenge the teachings with philosophical reasoning. Hid ideas were derived by reasoning, and it is this that marks Buddhism out as a philosophy as much as (perhapseven more than) a religion. In the Brahmanism of Gautama's time, the Hindu religion saw "Nirvana" (after many cycles of birth-death-birth) as becoming one with God, but Gautama carefully avoids any mention of a deity or of an ultimate purpose of life. He merely describes Nirvana as "unborn, unoriginated, uncreated, and uninformed", and transcending any sensory experience. It is an eternal and unchanging state of non-being, and so the ultimate freedom from suffering of existence. The preaching of Gautama Buddha was widely accepted across India, China, and Southeast Asia, and Buddhism got established as a religion.

Gautam Buddha's thoughts echoed in the thoughts of Western Philosophers. such as Hume's concept of the 'Self' and Schopenhauer's view of the human condition. But the major impact on the thinking of the western world happened only after the 20th century. Since then, more and more Westerners have turned to it for guidance on how to live.

Around the same time, Confucius (551-479BCE) a Philosopher in China, rose to prominence with his teachings compiled in "Analects". According to Analects, we humans are the agents of that heaven which has chosen us to embody its will and to unite the world with moral order. Thus, we see that concept of heaven is not recent but was prevalent even during the pre-historic times. The concept was put to use for bringing a sense of moral order in society.

Socrates (469-399BCE) is considered one of the founders of Western Philosophy. He preaches that we must "continually" examine our lives. He claimed that "evil" was done because of a lack of wisdom and knowledge. He concluded that there is only one good: knowledge. All knowledge is ultimately self-knowledge, for it creates the person you are within this world and fosters the care of the ***immortal soul.*** In *Phaedo,* Socrates says that an unexamined life leads the soul to be "confused and dizzy as if it were drunk", while the wise soul achieves stability, its straying is finally brought to an end.

Thus, we see that the idea of the "soul" and its reaching stability (In Buddhism) and recent religions calling it Nirvana; was prevalent even during 400 BC and is still being explored in our current times.

Plato (427-327 BCE) also talks about the "soul". He believes that human beings are divided into two parts: the body and the soul. Our body possesses the senses, through which we are able to perceive the material world, while the soul possesses the reason with which we can perceive the realm of ideas. Plato concludes that our soul, which is immortal and eternal, must have inhabited the world of Ideas before our birth, and still yearns to return to the realm after our death.

The thoughts of Plato around 350 BC are still relevant and we have not progressed much in the knowledge of soul, death, and the afterlife.

Athenian philosopher Epicurus (341-270BCE) reasons about the fear of death- He says that one obstacle to enjoying the peace of a tranquil mind is the fear of death., This fear is further enhanced by the religious belief that if you incur the wrath of gods, you will be severely punished in the afterlife. Epicurus, rather than countering this fear by proposing an alternative state of immortality, tries to explain the nature of death itself. He starts by proposing that when we die, we are unaware of our death since our consciousness (our soul) ceases to exist at the point of death. To explain this, Epicurus takes the view that the entire universe consists of either atoms or empty space, as argued by the atomist philosophers Democritus and Leucipuss. Epicurus then reasons the soul cannot be empty space, because it operates dynamically with the body, so it must be made up of atoms. He describes these atoms of the soul as being distributed around the body, but as being so fragile that they dissolve when we die, and so we are no longer capable of sensing anything. If you are unable to feel anything mentally or physically, when you die, it is foolish to let the fear of death cause you pain while you are still alive.

It is simply amazing to observe at the current time the thought process, the logic, and the reasoning of philosophers who lived in ancient times -300 BC. How his logic leads to a statement that death is painless, which is verified centuries later through Near-death experiences

(NDEs). In fact, NDEs tell us that experiencer of death has a joyous feeling at the time of death. Epicurus was right in proposing that it is foolish to fear death because death is painless!!

Coming to the era after Christ's death i.e., A.D.- Philosopher Avicenna from Uzbekistan proposed that the soul is distinct from the body. Avicenna was deeply influenced by the Philosophical thoughts of Aristotle, but he deviated from Aristotle on the topic of "soul". Aristotle was of the view that the body and mind of living entities are not different things (or substances), but one unit, and the mind is the "form" of the human body. As such, it is responsible for all the activities of a human being can perform. For this reason, Aristotle does not seem to think it possible for anything to survive the death of the body.

By contrast, Avicenna thinks that the body and the mind are two distinct substances. His great predecessor in this view was Plato who thought of the mind as a distinct thing that was imprisoned in the body. Plato believed that at the point of death, the mind would be released from its prison, to be later reincarnated in another body.

In seeking to prove the divided nature of mind and body, Avicenna devised a thought experiment known as "Flying Man". In the experiment, Avicenna wants to examine what we can know if we are effectively robbed of our senses and cannot depend on them for information. In the "Thought Experiment" Avicenna asks us each to imagine this: *Suppose I have just come into existence, but I have all my normal intelligence. Suppose, too, that I am floating in the air, and my limbs are separated from each other, so I can touch nothing. Suppose I am entirely without any sensation. Nonetheless, I am sure that I myself exist. But what is this self, which is me? It cannot be any of the parts of my body, because I do not know that I have any. The self that I affirm as existing does not have any length or breadth. It has no extension or physicality.*

It follows from this that the human self – what I am- is distinct from my body, or anything physical. The "Flying Man" experiment, says

Avicenna, is a way of alerting and reminding oneself of the existence of the mind as something other than, and distinct from, the body.

How fascinating!! While reading, now, these thoughts written in the tenth century made me feel that I was probably reinventing the wheel when I was writing a book titled, "The Brain, Mind, Consciousness and the vital question-Who am I". I thought it was innovative of me to delve into this topic which I thought no one had given much thought to. Not that there is nothing new in my book; it does contain the material which was not known in the 10th century as science was yet to advance but the very thought that " I" is different from my body parts was thought by Avicenna in the 10th century leaves me dumbstruck and gives me a feeling of reinventing the wheel.

Avicenna goes further to say that the intellectual knowledge the mind can grasp cannot be contained by anything material. It is easy to see how the parts of physically shaped things fit with the parts of a physical sense organ: the image of the wall that I see is stretched over the lens of my eye- the sense organ for sight. But the mind is not a sense organ, what it grasps are definitions. The mind therefore cannot be in any way like or part of the body. ***He goes on to suggest that the mind is not destroyed when the body dies and that it is immortal.***

Thus, we observe that even in the tenth century the knowledge that living things outlive life was in existence amongst the philosophers who were adept in logical thinking.

Later in 1640, Descartes returned with dualistic thought in line with Avicenna's thoughts- he says that he can be deceived about all the things but one thing he cannot be deceived about is that he exists. This self is exactly the self that Avicenna's "Flying man" is sure of when he has no other knowledge. Like Avicenna, Descartes concludes that the "I" or self is completely distinct from the body and that it must be immortal.

Today philosophers are divided between a small number of dualists and a large number of thinkers who say that the mind is simply the brain. Many philosophers, especially European thinkers accept the results of Avicenna's "Flying man" experiment in one central way that we, each, have a self with a first-person view of the world (the "I") that is not accommodated by the objective view of the scientific world.

In fact, today we have come much further in understanding the Brain and Mind. The brain is the functional correlate of mind and the mind has a correlation with Consciousness which is still a "hard problem" for modern scientists and thinkers. Modern-day Australian Philosopher David Chalmers points out that certain functions of consciousness-such as the use of language and the processing of information- can be explained in terms of the mechanisms that perform those functions, and that physicalist philosophers have been offering variants of this approach for centuries. However, the harder problem of explaining the nature of the subjective, first-person experience of consciousness remains unsolved by them. There seems to be a built-in mismatch between the objects of the physical sciences on one hand and the subjects of conscious experiences on the other.

Coming back to philosophers' thoughts across history, the thoughts of Avicenna are special and one thing that emerges from the thinking of Avicenna is that there is an entity distinct from the body and body parts—it could reside within or outside the physical body.

Jalal Ad-Din Muhammad Rumi (1207-1273 A.D.) thought that man is a link between the past and future in a continual process of life, death, rebirth—not as a cycle, but in a progression from one form to another stretching into eternity. Death and decay are inevitable and part of this endless flow of life, but as something ceases to exist in one form, it is reborn into another. Because of this, we should have no fear of death nor should we grieve a loss. The thoughts of Rumi are somewhat similar to eastern philosophical and religious thoughts on life, death, and reincarnation.

As we saw in the above paragraphs, the philosophers from the ages even before Christ have been propagating their views of the existence of life after death. The Bhagwad Geeta, an Indian religious book preaches that there is no death because the soul is immortal- death is just like changing clothes and the soul wears new cloth in the form of a new body by getting born after death.

The belief in after-life was necessary for mankind and this need made most religions believe in life after death. Hindu religion believes in life after death as found in the Bhagawad Geeta. The religions of different cultures have tried to deal with death--most have put forth a belief in the continuation of life after death e.g Christians and Islamic have evolved to be a believer in Personal Resurrection in distant future (Moreman 2006). It is only this belief, which, prevents Muslims to destroy the dead body by burning; instead, they bury the whole body so that on the "D" day of resurrection, their bodies will come to life.

Greek pyramids are testimonials of a belief that in the future, the dead will return to life and, hence, dead bodies are mummified.

The belief in after-life, thus, serves as an anchor for all religions. Have you ever thought that belief in after-life has helped mankind in many ways; I devote the following paragraphs to bring home this point:

Impact of belief on mankind

We see and witness the great impact of religious beliefs on people of different cultures. Muslims leave all work five times a day and face Mecca to pray; Americans make a weekly pilgrimage to the church.

Sentiments of people get hurt and cause violent aggression if something derogatory is hurled on their religious belief.

Look at the mental thought process of a suicide bomber terrorist or a soldier who is willing to sacrifice his life for a belief (about after-life). (Milgram (1974); Ross & Nisbett 1991).

Zimbardo (1969), suggests "Social psychology has shown that a strong belief of some reality motivates a person to do extraordinary things." For example- to the extent of sacrificing his own life.

The point I wish to make, is that the beliefs do have tremendous impact on contemporary lives, not only, on the believer, but also, on others, who get affected by the actions of the believer. Belief systems regulate our thought processes and actions.

A Survey was done for 1235 respondents in which respondents were asked the following 4 questions:

1. Only my physical body will die
2. My body is just a very temporary home for me
3. Death is just a new beginning
4. I believe in miracles.

the respondents were also asked to respond to other questions related to personality traits, demographic details, socio-religious beliefs, and other values. They were asked to rank the answers with scores from 1 to 5 in the following manner-The respondent got a score

Score 1-If his answer is that it is very uncharacteristic of me.

Score 2-If his answer is that it is uncharacteristic of me.
Score 3-If his answer is I am neutral about it.
Score 4-If the answer is that it is characteristic of me.
Score 5-If the answer is that it is very characteristic of me.

Thus, the score will vary between 4 and 20.

Evidently, the lowest score on the transcendental score would mean that the respondent is firmly against the belief of survival after death; and as the score goes up, he goes to become neutral to the belief (i.e score12, scoring 3 for each question) and then the rising scores indicate his growing belief in survival theory –score 20 meaning that he is a staunch believer in survival theory.

The analysis of data indicated that persons scoring high on the above scale constituted youngsters below the age of 20 or elders above the age of 50 and women were found to score higher than men when measured on this scale. The study also throws light on how the belief in survival impacts people's lives.

Influences of belief in Life after death on people

Important influences which appeared coming from a belief of survival theory (i.e from responses of who scored above 12 on the scale) were as follows:

1. The belief serves as positive reinforcement in current life-Nirvanic beliefs about transcendental-future make present inequities less painful.
2. Irrational acts viz cult members irrationally follow their leader and embrace death, they may not be ending life but maybe, rationally, moving towards their transcendental - future goals.
3. Suicide bombers are not sacrificing their lives for a cause but for a selfish motive of seeking personal gain in the afterlife ---here I want to recall a television interview, where a child aged 9-10 years of age, undergoing training in a terrorist training camp, is asked what great work he is going to do when he grows up. He replies that he is going to bombard a crowd and kill people. When asked what purpose will it serve –his answer is that it will lead him to a blissful/meaningful next life that will be full of enjoyment. A child's mind is tender and can be easily molded to any belief system. The belief of survival had influenced him so greatly on a transcendental scale that he was willing to forego all material gains in current worldly life, and looked forward to eternally soothing life beyond survival. I do not advocate that

intentions were good, but only, want to bring home the point that survival theory did have a deep impact on the mind of a child and he found a purpose in life that turned out to be destructive.

The next few paragraphs reveal some more purposes served by survival belief.

Survival theory concerning communication between deceased persons and living people i.e., After Death Communication **(ADC)** from deceased people, has had deep impacts on the lives of people who underwent the experience of after-death communication.

Krippner (2000) narrates Surveys that indicate a positive effect of ADC on experiments of ADC after connecting with the deceased loved ones. Devers (1994) in his study, claimed that the pain of loss of dear ones was greatly reduced with the belief of survival after ADC.

Berger (1995) found that the experiments, which believed in survival could easily come to terms with the loss of the deceased and return to normalized routines. Drewery(2003) found from 40 ADC reports that experiments reported relief, comfort, hope, encouragement, forgiveness, love, and joy when bereaved completed unfinished business left by the deceased.

ADC experiences and adaptive grief outcomes were investigated by Parker (2004) who interviewed 12 people, bereaved for less than one year. As was the case with most of the other investigators, she screened out psychiatric patients and those with obvious mental illness. Of the research participants, 11 experienced positive changes such as personal and/or spiritual growth. Their ADC experiences appeared to have played specific roles and to have fulfilled specific needs within the context of bereavement, especially when they were considered to be veridical in nature. Parker concluded that ADC experiences were not a sign of psychopathology, but, part of human experience.

Few counselors, psychiatrists, and psychological therapists have used ADCs, in one form or another, as part of what has become known as "bereavement therapy" or "grief therapy". For example, a procedure inducing "visitation" dreams has been developed by a well-known dream worker, Robert Moss (2005). His approach purports to enable bereaved people to dream about departed loved ones, attaining a closure that was not possible while they were alive.

It is found that after death communication instills a belief in survival and this belief in survival serves the following purposes in the life of experiments: -

1. ADC gives comfort and reassurance that the relationship continues even after death.
2. The experiments feel that they get protected from oncoming dangers because the deceased could pre-warn them about the same.
3. ADC provided them a sense of life purpose and meaning.
4. ADC confirmed the hope that there is life after death; e.g., the self is immortal and removed the fear of death.
5. Sometimes ADC helped to complete unfinished business giving great relief.
6. ADC changed the way of looking at life through reduced anger, guilt, and/or anxiety against the deceased.
7. The belief of survival gave a good feeling that the deceased loved him/ her and had not forgotten even when passed away.
8. ADC provided information hitherto unknown.
9. Helped survivors to make his /her own exit from the world easier and less painful.

Furthermore, the most important purpose of belief in survival is a therapeutic application of the belief.

LaGrand (1999) presented several ways, by which, ADC experience could be used in grief counseling. He emphasized that the critical view is not whether ADC can be confirmed or refuted but how this belief can be used to help people deal with the loss. The therapeutic approach, "Induced after-death communication", is developed by Botkin with Hogan (2005). They advocated "Inducing" ADCs with the Eye Movement Desensitization & Reprocessing Modality (EMDR), a therapeutic modality, often used to treat veterans suffering from post-traumatic stress disorder.

Let us now look at another aspect of survival theory that influences our lives greatly. Freud (1915/1962) says, "In the unconscious, every one of us is convinced of his /her immortality. Our unconscious does not believe in its own death, it believes as if it is immortal." Indian Philosophy also talks about the inner self "soul" being immortal Concept of "Immortality of self" emerging out from the theory of survival has brought peace in the minds of people. We all know that fear of any kind makes us highly uncomfortable and the feeling makes us shiver. Fear is having a stunning impact because we are anticipating something ghastly to happen which is not known to us. Once we become aware of the unknown, the fear loses its impact. The concept of immortality brings this awareness, thus, reducing the impact of fear and making us live life normally.

Mythological narratives typically address existential human issues and have consequences for behavior; they may be cultural, institutional, ethnic, familial, and/or personal in nature. Until science develops the technology to confirm or falsify the "survival hypothesis," it is up to the experiments to dismiss them as "exceptional experiences" that are curious but unimportant anomalies or to construct them into "exceptional human experiences" and revel in their transformative power.

As for the mythological narratives---the great purpose served by believing in the afterlife, mythologically, is available in Indian Holy Book, "Bhagavad Gita", which has become the base of Indian Philosophy.

In the ancient epic battle of Mahabharata, King Arjuna, seeing his own cousins and uncles in the enemy army, felt sad and disheartened and was not the usual brave self, because, he did not see any meaning in winning back his kingdom if he has to kill his own relatives for that. He put down his arrow and bows and declared to Lord Krishna that he won't fight the battle, because, he won't be able to enjoy the victory over the dead bodies of his own cousins and uncles.

Here came the preaching of Lord Krishna to Arjuna which is captured in form of verses in the holy book "Bhagavad Gita" and has become the heart and soul of Indian Philosophy. Gita has been interpreted differently by writers all over the world and people are greatly influenced by the philosophical interpretation of the verses. Each couplet has embedded philosophy and gives meaning to our life and death and registers our belief in life after death. The impact of this belief is great!

The essence of His preaching is summarized –

He preaches to Arjuna the meaning of death and life and cycles of life-death and death-life. He explains to Arjuna the meaning of death by saying, "Do not be deterred by fear of death of relatives because in reality there is no "death". We are indestructible, our physical body perishes but not we. We just change into another body on bodily death in the same way as we, in our current life, change our clothes."

He exhorts Arjuna to behave like a warrior (Kshatriya) and do his duty as a warrior. Everything is pre-destined; you have to do only your duty and not to bother about results or consequences because these are not in your hands. The fruits of your actions will come automatically and there is no use worrying about the fruits of your deeds since you can't help it."

The divine words on the belief of "survival after death", had a great impact on Arjuna who is enlightened with survival belief which removes shock of thought of death from his mind and removes his guilt as he is not the doer of any action because nothing is in his hands and his life is only for doing his duty and not for looking for fruits of his doings.

The survival belief does serve the purpose and the Warrior Arjuna goes into the battle and proves to the world, the universal truth that there is always the victory of good over evil.

The above discussions clearly show that the belief in life after death does serve many purposes, some of which, concern the bereaved persons who get comfort by overcoming the grief of the loss of dear ones and continue their normal life. The belief overcomes the fear of oncoming death through awareness of immortality of self, thereby, makes way for peaceful exit during bodily death. The belief instills sense of purpose in life, gives comfort and reassurance that the relationship continues even after death. Not only that this belief can be put to therapeutic use to alleviate the sufferings of people from traumatic illnesses. It impacts a large number of people and even impacts various cultures because the belief is a strong motivator for our actions and behaviour.

We do not know whether there is life after death but even a belief that it does exist serves many purposes to help mankind. But the question remains whether we outlive death.

The materialistic view opposes this thought and maintains that life ceases to exist when we die and there is no further manifestation of life in any other form after the body dies. The body is like a machine and when it stops and is beyond repairs it is scrapped and that is the end of the body and life. There are thinkers who believe that the existing laws of science cannot accommodate the view that there is some form of life continuance after death.

Caroll M Sean (2013) has the following arguments:

“We know better for life after death, although people are much more reluctant to admit it. Admittedly, "direct" evidence one way or the other is hard to come by -- all we have are a few legends and sketchy claims from unreliable witnesses with near-death experiences, plus a bucketload of wishful thinking. But surely, it's okay to take account of indirect evidence -- namely, compatibility of the idea that some form of our individual soul survives death with other things we know about how the world works.

Claims that some form of consciousness persists after our bodies die and decay into their constituent atoms face one huge, insuperable obstacle: the laws of physics underlying everyday life are completely understood, and there's no way within those laws to allow for the information stored in our brains to persist after we die. If you claim that some form of soul persists beyond death, what particles is that soul made of? What forces are holding it together? How does it interact with ordinary matter?

Everything we know about Quantum Field Theory (QFT) says that there aren't any sensible answers to these questions. Of course, everything we know about quantum field theory could be wrong. Among advocates for life after death, nobody even tries to sit down and do the hard work of explaining how the basic physics of atoms and electrons would have to be altered for this to be true. If we tried, the fundamental absurdity of the task would quickly become evident. Even if you don't believe that human beings are "simply" collections of atoms evolving and interacting according to rules laid down in the Standard Model of particle physics, most people would grudgingly admit that atoms are *part* of who we are. If it's really nothing but atoms and the known forces, there is clearly no way for the soul to survive death. Believing in a life after death, to put it mildly, requires physics beyond the Standard Model. Most importantly, we need some way for that "new physics" to interact with the atoms that we do have.

Very roughly speaking, when most people think about an immaterial soul that persists after death, they have in mind some sort of blob of spirit energy that takes up residence near our brain and drives around our body like a soccer mom driving an SUV. The questions are these: what form does that spirit energy take, and how does it interact with our ordinary atoms? Not only is new physics required, but dramatically new physics. Within QFT, there can't be a new collection of "spirit particles" and "spirit forces" that interact with our regular atoms, because we would have detected them in existing experiments. Ockham's razor is not on your side here, since you have to posit a completely new realm of reality obeying very different rules than the ones we know."

The sentiments put up against the thought of life outliving death are hard-hitting and these go against the belief system of believers in after-life.

The aspect of life after death is complicated and as the above arguments posit, the current laws of science can't accommodate the idea of life after death. But science does evolve with new discoveries and we do not know the future!

The Proponents argue that if there is no life after death then how do we account for apparitions of deceased people seen by live people. Lincoln's apparition cited at beginning of the chapter is a live example. There are many real-life incidences found in literature: Erica Simon narrates innumerable real-life incidents that point to the continuation of life after death, where the discarnate spirits have appeared as apparitions to their living relatives.

Literature is full of real-life instances where after death communications (ADCs) happened, re-incarnation was confirmed, apparitions were seen by live people. We do not have any scientific explanation for such events. Survival theory explains them as entities who are wandering in search of their rebirth. There is birth after death i.e., reincarnation takes place and the cycle of birth-life-death-birth-life… goes on

However, there are some theories that try to explain after-death communications (ADCs) from a point of view which is different from believing in life after death.

Super psi Theory

Braude(2003) claims, that, Super psi theory can give a better alternative explanation to so-called survival incidents depicting after-death communications. He goes on to say, "In most areas of science, fundamental philosophical assumptions, usually, form part of the received conceptual background. But in the case of survival research, deep philosophical issues dominate the foreground. Many have wondered whether the very ***concept*** of survival is intelligible. And as the reader may realize, some have decided that it is not, and have therefore argued that we should reject the survival hypothesis a ***priori*** (see, Flew, 1976)."

It will be, too harsh and abrupt, to reject the hypothesis on such a weak logic, but, what if, an alternate hypothesis can explain the so-called survival incidents in a more easy and plausible way.

In Survival theory relating to after-death communication (ADC), the experiencer, comes to know about something, hitherto, unknown to him, through communication from a discarnate person(deceased, returning after death)----could it not be due to Medium's super psi ability to see beyond normal and get to know the details through the very refined and advanced psi ability (Super psi) i.e., learning the details, without interaction with the spirit of deceased, as propagated by Survival theory. Sudduth (2009) believes that the most serious obstacle, to taking even the best evidence for survival at face value, is the possibility that the data can be explained in terms of highly-refined psi (Super psi) among the living.

We, often, assume that, if psi occurs, it can occur only up to a modest degree. Why so, we, simply, have no grounds for placing antecedent limits of any kind, on its scope or refinement. If, "psi," can occur at all, then until we have evidence to the contrary, we must assume that it can occur at any level of magnitude or sophistication. In fact, not only, do we have no evidence against the possibility of unlimited psi, but, certain bodies of data actually support it. So-called Mediums can be examples of people possessing a high level of psi ability (super psi ability), (Braude, 1986).

Since, we, presently, have no grounds for imposing any antecedent limits on the scope or refinement of psychic functioning, we cannot deny the possibility of having access to information only through the medium's super psi ability, how he uses the ability; is immaterial, and, we need not bother about it -it is, just, an extension of psievent, and that's it.

In order to dwell on the subject further, Sudduth (2009) defines ***M evidence.***

Data collected from mediumship constitute important evidence – called, "***M evidence.***"

M evidence includes significant veridical information about the life of some deceased person(s), possessed by the medium, and communicated to the sitter. Mediums acquire knowledge of various facts, ostensibly, originating from the deceased personality, especially, knowledge of events or activities in the lives of friends and family of the deceased. *M* evidence also includes data about, how, this veridical information is communicated to the sitter by the medium. *M* evidence, also, includes various physical phenomena frequently alleged to occur in séance settings (for example, materializations, levitations,).

It is widely held that the mediumship attributes some degree of psychic functioning to medium, but survivalist believe that the discarnate spirit has influence over the medium by psychic means i.e., it is not medium who use normal psi but the ***discarnate spirit***.

Whereas, the super-psi hypothesis attempts to explain *M* evidence, solely, in terms of psychological and paranormal resources at the command of medium i.e there is no role of discarnate spirits, just because the medium possesses super psi ability, the manifestation of M evidence takes place.

After death communication, (a prominent aspect of survival after death) leading us to believe in life after death is very convincingly explained by Super psi theory which does not believe in life after death. But this theory does not explain the incidents of appearance of apparitions of ghosts/spirits which are often seen by people and there are people called "Mediums" who have a special ability to call them to manifest before us.

Can apparitions or manifestation of spirits be explained without taking the help of belief in life after death? The following paragraphs are devoted to examining this aspect:

Probably we see apparitions/ spirits because of aberration of working of our brain.

Ghosts / Apparitions could be hallucinatory and caused by brain aberrations:

Appearances of ghosts and apparitions have been baffling mankind. However, there are views that these are not appearing in reality but may be resulting due to some aberrations of mind.

Canadian neuroscientist, Michael Persinger, had demonstrated that the application of electromagnetic field to temporal lobes of the brain could provide haunting experience viz: perception of a presence of a person, or, a sensation of touch, when, in reality, there is no presence or no one has touched.

Mr. Shange and his team from Clarkson University in US, observed that fungal pores can cause a perception of haunting.

Supernatural perception can also arise from the brain's reaction to toxic substances -such as carbon mono-oxide, formaldehyde, and pesticide. It is also suggested that fungal hallucinations caused by the toxic mold could stimulate haunting-related perceptions. This may explain why ghosts sighting, often, seems to occur in older buildings. This means that toxic molds can trigger significant mental or neurological symptoms which create perceptions, similar to, those reported during haunting experiences.

Pareidolia is another phenomenon where the mind is wrongly perceiving things---normal as well as Paranormal. Let us understand what Pareidolia is

Pareidolia is defined as a psychological phenomenon that causes people to see patterns in a random stimulus. This often leads to people assigning human characteristics to objects.

Susana Martinez Conde (2018) maintains that human brains are attuned to perceive faces – an entire region of the brain, called Fusiform Gyrus, is dedicated to it. The face detection skill by this portion of the brain, coupled with, our brain's compulsion to extract meanings from the sensory chaos that surrounds us, drives us to see faces where there aren't any.

Pareidolia can also result in the perception of two things from a single image. This visual illusion created by Pareidolia can be experienced by looking intently at a painting entitled "My wife and mother in law" by W E Hill. You will either see a young woman looking away or the profile of an old woman: two perceptions contained in the same picture. The picture is reproduced below:

Pareidolia is often taken as a logical explanation for apparitions seen in vague forms in a low illuminating environment.

So, we, now, have some explanation about after-death communication and for apparitions without leaning to the theory that life exists after death.

The question is whether are these credible and scientific? Can these be taken as proof that life does not exist after death?

Prima facie-super psi theory is not acceptable in mainstream science as psi is an aspect of Parapsychology and Parapsychology is still not considered as scientific; the reasons have been discussed in the first chapter.

Pareidolia could be true in some cases where apparitions appeared in an environment that had dim light. Wrong perception/pareidolia cannot be true en-block for all apparitions or ghosts. These can be isolated cases but cannot be true universally for all cases.

Also, it will amount to stretching logic too far to believe that all haunting cases are experienced only in old dilapidated buildings; also, there may be instances where Pareidolia was absent, but, still anomalous made its presence.

Hence the above arguments do explain partially but are not a piece of strong evidence that there is no life after death.

Even the theories supporting and opposing the belief of life after death (viz., survival theory and super psi theory) do not explain many bizarre incidents related to life after death being observed all over the world.

The Super psi theory does not touch many aspects relevant to life after death. While occurrences of post-mortem knowledge of previous incidents (got through séances) could be explained through Super psi but how do cases of visible apparitions be explained. Even when these are not visible to living humans, their presence is marked by animals like dogs, cats, and rattlesnakes. Erica Simon (2006) writes, "Animals often do react to apparitions---quite often with fear."

Reincarnation is another area that is not touched by Super psi Theory. Instances of reincarnations are overwhelming. Stevenson's whole life's work speaks volumes about it but this theory does not touch upon this intriguing phenomenon.

There are many more questions needing answers from both the theories- both the theories are confined to human life; what happens to non-human lives – whether these survive death or their journey stops here?

Scientists have found signs of life on Mars. There can be life in many planets of the Universe; their life forms are not yet known -whether they resemble humans or have different forms is not known. What would be happening to their lives, once they meet death?

Furthermore, could there be transmigration across planets when death manifests? Could it be possible that after death, the post-death human forms manifest in life as non-human species or vice-versa within earth planet or across the Cosmos? If we outlive death, do we take birth as humans or do we get born in other species?

If a cycle of birth-death-birth happens, how do we come out of the confusion of identity crisis?

Also, both theories do not have any scientific foundation.

Energy Survival theory proposed by me finds answers to the above questions and also the theory is built on a scientific foundation of Energy transformations:

Energy Survival Theory

The theory is being based on the scientific truth that Energy cannot be created or destroyed; it, only, changes form. My paper – "***Life after Death-Contemporary Theories and Beyond***" gives scientific details about Energy Forms and their transformations, explains the difference between physical energy and subtle energy and states the law of conservation of energy. The theory is built on the above concepts and has a foundation in the scientific law of conservation of energy.

The theory stands on concepts of two energy forms; one of them is the physical-***Self Life Energy Form (SLEF)*** and the other is the subtle energy form -***Individual Self Energy Form (ISEF)***. ISEF is a unique eternal subtle energy form that goes on transforming to different SLEFs with different physical identities but the ISEF has a unique identity. SLEF loses its identity on physical death and at physical death, this energy form gets transformed back to its unique energy form ISEF. The reincarnation of SLEF takes place when its unique ISEF gets transformed into SLEF with a different physical identity. Thus, the cycle of energy transformations ISEF-SLEF-ISEF-SLEF.... goes on and in this physical world, the same is known as the cycle of birth-death-birth-death... As per this theory, all living entities are getting transformations from ISEF to SLEFs and back. Humans don't need to get transformed again as humans, they may get transformation as humans or even as non-human living forms. They can be reborn on this earth or any other planet in the universe.

The physical energy SLEF is governed by physical scientific laws whereas the subtle energy is not.

For example, we cannot see subtle energy-Why are we not able to see Subtle Energy fields? Human senses operate within a narrow range in the electromagnetic spectrum, the measurable band of energy that produces various types of light. Our eyes can only detect radiation, the term for noticeable energy emitted by substances, in the range of 380 to 780 nanometres. That is visible light. Infra-red light, which we cannot see, has a wavelength of 1000 nanometres, and far-ultraviolet light operates at 200 nanometers. We cannot see what we are not capable to see.

Subtle Energy moves at a fast speed and has no mass, we do not currently have the equipment needed to measure them but this does not mean that what is invisible does not exist. The micro-organisms which could not be seen by the eye, needed microscopes to prove that they exist. Similarly, Subtle energy exists but is invisible to the eye.

Subtle energies operate by different rules than measurable energies. The subtle energy rules for the subtle structures are encoded with ideas from quantum physics, the study of energetic interactions on the micro-levels. Subtle energies, rule-breakers as they are, can stretch --- and sometimes completely ignore---time and space, change form at will, and occupy many places at one time.

Another unique characteristic of subtle energies is that within the subtle structures, they not only adjust the physical world but, also adjust to it."

The subtle Energy form ISEF is eternal and while getting transformed into SLEF remain connected to SLEF by a retractable field or energy commonly referred to as "Silver cord" ----*Robert Crookall(1977) – The study and practice of Astral Projection.*

The silver cord acts as a leash on our physical body(as per me it is SLEF) in that it prevents it from getting lost in the outer realms or fails to return to the physical body; the silver cord performs as an intermediary between the physical body(SLEF) & Subtle energy form(I call it ISEF), broken only at the time of Biological demise— At that time, however, the non-physical body (ISEF), which houses the consciousness, departs to begin a new phase of existence between physical lives obtained by further transformations at new birth cycles as physical bodies. The period between transformation to the non-physical body (The subtle energy form) to retransformation to the new physical body is termed as 'the intermissive period".

The "silver cord", often referred to as one's bio-energy or energetic body; is the connection point through which the fields of energy flow back and forth between physical (SLEFs) and non-physical bodies (ISEFs). This constant exchange of energy is necessary in order to maintain the function of our body whether in a physical state or outside the physical state in a non-physical state. It also enables a non-physical state (ISEF) to travel great distances from its physical counterpart (SLEF). In the intermissive period, ISEF can travel to distant places and get transformed to a new Life form SLEF and get localized at that place temporarily till SLEF again transforms back to ISEF, which is then free to move out anywhere.

The Silver cord remains intact till death occurs. At death, the cord snaps, and transformation take place from Physical form to Subtle Energy form and ISEF becomes free to move into ethereal space.

While the Subtle energy form has a transformation in physical form, it does preserve its traces of subtle nature in form of Aura surrounding the physical body. In Energy Survival theory we can say that ISEF (the subtle energy form) is present eternally and the Life form SLEF comes into being when sperm and egg of living species unite but the egg fertilization happens only when ISEF (the subtle energy form) gets entangled in sperm and egg bondage and loses its subtle form and its transformation happens to live energy form SLEF, though, the traces of Subtle form remains in form of Aura surrounding SLEF and after death, this aura retains the shape of its SLEF and appears on some occasions as ghost/ spirit to humans of the world.

At death, the new physical form SLEF, gets a new physical entity with a new name and will add to the knowledge in ISEF which already has an accumulation of knowledge from previous SLEFs who were entangled with it in past. The new Physical form will be known by a different name in the physical world. In this perpetual cycle, ISEF, continues to evolve further and gets on getting refined through the various life cycles and goes on adding more and more knowledge, the Manifestation of which comes to us in witnessing learned wizards, like Eienstein, Newton, and the like appearing on the earth.

SLEF once manifested as a physical body after transformation happens from ISEF to SLEF dies and reverse transformation SLEF to ISEF happens. And then in the life-death-life cycle, the SLEF manifests again as a different person when ISEF re transforms into SLEF. Since the accumulated knowledge/intelligence and memory gets stored in ISEF, in the new life the memories are accessible from the ISEF, and in rare cases, the new life form does get access to it and we have the phenomenon of ***Reincarnation***.

Communication is another intriguing factor and we shall deal with it now.

Communication between Energy forms

ISEF when transformed to SLEF, the Physical form will communicate with other live SLEF using the known five senses.

But how communication happens when it transforms into the latent dormant state as ISEF, when the Individual Energy Form has achieved a timeless, space-less feat that transcends long distances with limitless boundaries of time and space. It may be hung in the cosmos or may have landed on a different planet. In an invisible subtle energy state, it does have accumulated knowledge gained through its several life forms. How sometimes the knowledge gets transmitted to living humans as after-death communication is a vital question!!

The subtle nature of the energy form ISEF, by definition is capable of transcending long distances and capable of energy transference, hence, communication to another ISEF having dormant energy form is possible for obvious reasons. But rarely there is a leak from Subtle energy form ISEF to other SLEFs and this comes as discarnate communications or ADCs (After death communications). there is a possibility of a leak of information from ISEF which is received by other SLEFs---how that leak happens is a subject matter currently not known.

Communication between ISEF to Non-human SLEF will not be intelligible to us and, hence, is not discussed.

As you must have observed that the Energy Survival Theory explains many questions not answered by other theories.

How Energy Survival Theory answers questions that remain unanswered by other theories

Let us once again recall the unanswered questions and see how the Energy Survival Theory answers them:

The theories are on philosophical plain and do not have a scientific foundation---***Energy Survival Theory is based on the scientific law of conservation of energy***

Radical Survivalism theory talks about Absolute knowledge form—what happens with this form? Does it get manifested in future forms? The theory does not explain reincarnation and the cycle of birth-death-birth… ***Energy Survival theory dwells on and explains reincarnation in details***

The appearance of discarnate spirits/ghosts is not explained by theories other than Survival Theory—***The concept of aura around SLEF appears as spirits/ghosts as per Energy Survival theory and is vividly explained.***

The theories do not talk about life after death for non-human living forms. – ***Energy Survival theory discusses all living forms***

What about the living forms existing in planets other than earth; what happens to them? – ***The ISEFs may be scattered across all planets and SLEFs may also reside on earth and other planets***

Where do we go after death? Are we confined to earth or we go to other planets in the cosmos? Can we traverse anywhere in the cosmos if we outlive death? –***Energy Survival theory discusses this at length***

If we outlive death, do we take birth as humans or do we get born in other species? –***Yes, as per Energy Survival Theory we can get born in other species including the one in which past life was enjoyed.***

If the cycle of birth-death-birth happens, how do we come out of the confusion of identity crisis--- ***ISEF has a unique identity (some sort of UIN-unique identification name) and is linked to numerous SLEFs which manifest in different transformed forms with a different name. Their bond is with unique ISEF so there is no identity crisis/ confusion***

So, we observe that Energy Survival Theory has answers to all questions which were left unanswered by other Theories on Life after

Death. However, few more questions which had not surfaced earlier are now confronting this Energy Survival theory:

- The Energy Survival Theory does not discuss the structure which holds ISEF and SLEFs together. It tells about silver cords which serve as a bond between unique ISEF and its several SLEFs but does not enlighten us about the bond between different SLEFs or between different ISEFs
- The Energy does not get created nor can it be destroyed, then, how come the SLEFs -the physical living forms, the persons are increasing in numbers as we see that the population on earth is increasing day by day. How does The Energy Survival Theory explain this?
- It does talk about communication between different SLEFs happening through the known five senses. But it is silent about communications observed between humans (a part of SLEFs) without the use of known five senses—the communications observed as in Telepathy or Clairvoyance, etc.
- It is not able to answer convincingly about the communications received from so-called spirits /ghosts i.e., the ISEFs auras to living human beings—i.e., the so-called after-death communications
- It is silent about communication between different ISEFs—whether they communicate; whether there is a need for them to communicate between themselves and if yes, how do they communicate?
- It tells about ISEF entering the living things when fertilization takes place in living females—is fertilization caused by the entry of ISEF into the body or is independent of it i.e., do ISEFs enter after fertilization or their entry is the cause of fertilization?
- Energy Survival Theory is silent about the conscious experience which happens at the time of death either by the then live SLEF or its unique ISEF

To answer these questions there is a need to expand the Energy Survival Theory which will increase its credibility and acceptability amongst critics and thinkers. The Energy Survival theory is extended and I present below the Extended Energy Survival Theory:

Extended Energy Survival Theory

The Energy Survival Theory has its foundation in the Law of Conservation of Energy which states that Energy cannot be created or destroyed, it can only undergo transformations.

We defined two Energy forms-ISEF and SLEF which we have discussed in detail. What we have not discussed is their structure and location in the Cosmos and how these forms are connected. We discussed one getting transformed into another but we do not know the correlation between different ISEFs and correlations between SLEFs of different ISEFs i.e., we know the bond between an ISEF and all its manifested SLEFs but we do not know the correlation existing between different SLEFs of other ISEFs. The more we question, the more complex become the issues.

To make it simpler let us discuss the basic structure comprising the two energy forms, the location of the structure in the cosmos, and the interconnection between the two energy forms.

There may be basically two classes of structures -one of ISEF and another of SLEF. Thematic picture giving the structures is given below:

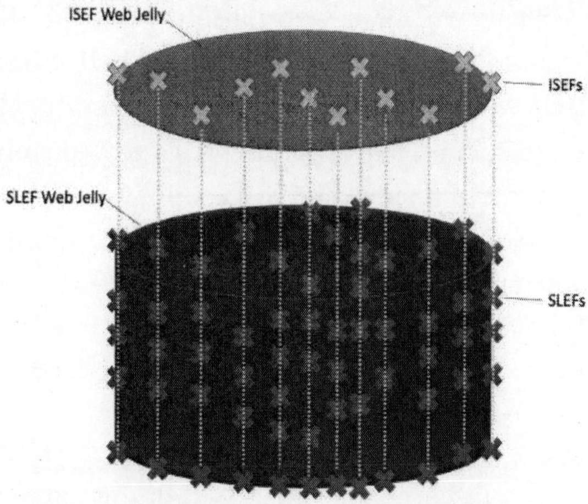

Thematic picture showing ISEF & SLEF Web Jellies connected with Silver cords

ISEF Structure

ISEF structure will be an infinitely large cob-web type jelly in which all ISEFs (which in SLEF forms could be humans/ insects/ animals ....) are embedded as points. The ISEFs are subtle energies that will not be different for different species. Only when it transforms into SLEF it may manifest physically as humans or animals or insects etc.... The ISEFs which are infinitely finite are all embedded in cob-web type jelly and hence are all connected. These are in a plane which is hung in cosmos much above the planets where SLEFs will manifest, meaning thereby that the plane of cobweb type jelly structure of ISEFs is located much above the cylindrical structure of cobweb jellies corresponding to SLEFs linked to unique ISEF through a hanging chain of silver cords. The different transformations of ISEF to SLEF will be hanging as a link.

All SLEFs corresponding to one ISEF will form a linked chain, and the SLEFs are connected to the unique ISEF through an elastic silver cord. The silver cord has to be elastic because newer and newer manifestations over time scale will go on adding to the unique ISEF, thus, making the chain becoming longer and longer maybe going infinitely long as time is infinite.

For each ISEF there will be a web jelly-like structure in which all SLEFs connected to ISEF through a silver cord are embedded. Such SLEF web jellies will be infinitely finite in numbers and there will be one SLEF web jelly for each ISEF in which all transformed SLEFs linked to the ISEF will reside. The SLEFs of an ISEF may have had physical form as human in one life and may have manifestation as an animal /insect or even human in another life as SLEF. So, the SLEF web Jelly will have all living forms-humans and non-humans. Since ISEF are infinitely finite in numbers, there will be an infinitely finite number of SLEF jellies.

The link of silver cords for one ISEF will go on extending as time passes its length is infinitely elongated with the passage of time.

Structure of SLEF Jellies and their location in the cosmos

Since the SLEFs will go on adding to the silver cord with each SLEF transformation over time, the chain linked to the ISEF plane will go on becoming longer. Thus, we cannot imagine the structure of SLEFs in one plane as thought about ISEF structure. Maybe we could have infinitely finite planes comprising of large periods of time, ordered serially as per passage of time. The conglomerate of the time planes would give it a form of cylindrical shape which is depicted in the thematic picture given above. The SLEF jellies of each ISEF will rest inside a big jelly mass of the overall cylindrical structure which has in its lap all the SLEFs manifested over a period of time and still continuing to manifest through energy transformations.

Another dimension is the location of SLEFs Structure. The huge cylindrical cobweb jelly type mass corresponding to SLEF will encompass all the planets where life exists because the SLEFs can get manifested on any planet. Each SLEF (may be human or non-human) chained in a silver cord will remain in the cylindrical jelly as a mere point.

Since the mass is jelly-like, it should be possible to have subset of jellies formed as per the living species— jelly could get formed encompassing all humans and also possible to get jellies corresponding to any non-human species. Whatever subset jellies are there the basic silver cord chain will remain intact and the jellies could get submerged into one another. The jelly-like structure makes it possible for all ISEFs and SLEFs to remain connected thru jelly-like mass. The entities are connected as well as insulated from each other by some unknown mechanism of insulation.

While concluding the structural aspects of the Energy Survival Theory, it will not be out of place to admit that the idea that we (the energy forms) are all connected and exist in web-like jelly was inspired by the thought process of Dean Radin laid down in his book, Entangled Minds(pp263,264):

It's as though we lived in a gigantic bowl of clear Jell-O. Every wiggle-every movement, event, and thought within that medium is felt throughout the bowl. Except, that this particular form of Jell-O is a rather peculiar medium, in that it's not localized in the usual way, nor is it squishy like ordinary Jell-O. It extends beyond the bounds of ordinary space-time, and it's not even a substance in the usual sense of the word.

Because of this "Non-local Jell-O" in which we are embedded, we can get glimpses of information about other people's minds, distant objects, or the future or past. We get this not through the ordinary known senses and not because of signals from those other minds and objects travel to our brain. But because at some level, our mind/brain is already co-existent with other people's minds, distant objects, and everything else. To navigate through this space, we use attention and intention. From this perspective, psychic experiences are reframed not as mysterious 'powers of the mind" but as momentary glimpses of the entangled fabric of reality. Particles that are quantum entangled do not imply that signals pass through them. Entanglement means that separated systems. Psi, on the other hand, seems to involve information transfer, like signal passing. At first glance, that seems to eliminate quantum correlations as an explanation of psi. However, that may not be true, it could be that it does not require information transfer at all. Maybe it's purely relational and manifests only as correlations. Maybe our bodies, minds, and brains are entangled in a holistic universe"

Could it be possible that the exchange of information between ISEF and live entities SLEFs a do not take help of signals but the information already manifests in us (being a part of a single entity where all of us are interconnected) the manifestation of information is blocked by insulations which if removed makes us fetch the information instantaneously?

It may sound absurd what I am hinting at. Maybe we are not discrete entities, we, the energy entities ISEFs and SLEFs are particles in the interconnected universe with some form of blockages or insulations that make us appear discrete and we act as though we are discrete. All information is there in the single entity ISEF of which we are only transformations. The revelation comes in a way similar to the observer effect—a mechanism of which is beyond the current understanding of science. The signals are not needed as the information already exists in the single entity which connects us all. The information flow is always there like the flow of electricity but cannot be felt. We get its feel like a shock when insulation (the blockage) gets removed.

In fact, all known energy forms have an insulation mechanism. Electrical energy gets insulation over the wire in which current flows, and the electrical current flow is made safe. Thermal Energy can also be insulated which prevents heat transfer to external surfaces which can be seen in thermal flasks and even the houses are insulated from heat or cold. We have insulation around nuclear reactors to prevent leakage of nuclear energy. Chemical energy results from chemical reactions between atoms or molecules and we could create insulation so that chemical reactions do not harm us.

Thus, we see that insulation serves as a safety measure for the known energy forms.

The same way the subtle energies and physical energies would have safety mechanisms in form of insulation. Insulation between ISEF and SLEF makes the world safe for us to live in; if there would be no insulation there would be chaos.

However, as we know that the communication between live contemporary SLEFs happens through the known five senses, and information flow is thus regulated between live contemporary living beings. But insulation between them prevents all communications without the use of the normal five senses. However, the bizarre psi phenomenon like Telepathy, etc. between live SLEFs do manifest and these could be due to the breach of the insulation.

The insulation breach between current live SLEFs and their ISEFs or with other ISEFs also takes place. Even a slight momentary insulation breach makes us shiver when SLEF is able to get the manifestation of its earlier SLEF (embedded in ISEF)—***Reincarnation;*** or SLEF gets manifestation of SLEF (of another ISEF) as apparition or ghost.

We are wonderstruck with these rare and momentary bizarre incidents which are results of insulation breach between the energy forms.

Currently, we do not know about the blockages or insulations which make us appear as discrete individual forms and the ways the blockages or insulations get breached.

Maybe more work on Quantum Entanglement can lead us to reach a scientific basis for Energy Survival Theory and we have a scientific explanation of death and the afterlife if we could research

and find out the mechanism of insulation/ blockage removal and reconnection.

Keeping the above-defined structures in view, the extended Energy Survival theory could take on the unanswered questions in Energy Survival Theory.

Let us take those questions one by one and try to find answers:

First unanswered question: The Energy Survival Theory does not discuss the structure which holds ISEF and SLEFs together. It tells about silver cords which serve as a bond between unique ISEF and its several SLEFs but does not enlighten us about the bond between different SLEFs or between different ISEFs--- ***the above discussions clarify all these points.***

The jelly-like structures because of the jelly-like nature keep all the SLEFs connected, the same way all ISEFs are connected. The connection between ISEF and SLEF is through the silver cords. There is some sort of insulation in the silver cord that prevents information flow between SLEFs corresponding to one ISEF. However, all information flows from SLEFs to its corresponding ISEF but this information flow is only one way. In rare instances, some breach of insulation does occur for a brief period and information flow happens instantaneously which appears bizarre—e.g., Telepathy; so, called after-death communication, or incarnate information.

The next unanswered question was: The Energy does not get created nor can it be destroyed, then, how come the SLEFs -the physical living forms-the persons are increasing in numbers as we see that the population on earth is increasing day by day. How does The Energy Survival Theory explain this?

The answer is evident if one studies the Energy Survival Theory deeply. We are led to this question as it is natural for us to think in terms of a human being alone. The theory talks about all living forms and even of those energy forms that have not lived at the moment. We are also not restricting to energy entities on our earth planet but even on other planets. If we take the sum total of all live SLEFs and add to them the ISEFs which currently are in subtle form, the figure which we shall arrive at will be infinitely finite and will be constant and not change at any time. Some live species may be increasing and others decreasing; even the ISEF numbers in waiting for the transformation will be changing but the sum total at any point in time will be constant.

Even when we consider only the planet earth, we find that the human population is not constant but in fact, it is increasing from time immemorial. This is because of the survival instinct prevalent in the human species, which is not so much prevalent in other species, which results in the extinction of many species—dinosaurs and alike have disappeared whereas their vacuum is filled by an increase in the human population. More and more living species from the earth and other planets are becoming extinct and their SLEFs through ISEFs are getting transformed into human SLEFs. The sum total of all Energy forms (Live SLEF+ Untransformed ISEF at any moment) is unchanging. They remain constant, thereby, they do not violate the law of conservation of Energy

Next question: It does talk about communication between different SLEFs happening through the known five senses. But it is silent about communications observed between humans (a part of SLEFs) without the use of known five senses—the communications observed as in Telepathy—*All live SLEFs being embedded in jelly-like mass are connected but are insulated from each other which prevents information/ communication flow and in normal situations but in rare occasions, there is momentary breach of insulation(due to unknown reasons) and information communication flow is instantaneous and there is a manifestation of telepathic communications.*

Further unanswered question: It is not able to answer convincingly about the communications received from so-called spirits /ghosts i.e., the ISEFs auras to living human beings—i.e., the so-called after-death communications--- *Using the same logic as above, the currently live and the subtle SLEFs(as ISEF which possesses all information about past life) are connected through the insulated silver cord which prevents information flow from ISEF to SLEF and normally we do not know about past SLEF's information but in a rare breach of insulation in the silver cord (reason Unknown) the information of past life from ISEF flows to the current live transformed SLEF and after-death communication manifests*

Next unanswered question: It is silent about communication between different ISEFs—whether they communicate; whether there is a need for them to communicate between themselves and if yes, how do they communicate? --- *Yes, communications indeed take place when the need arises; we do not know whether there is any need for communication between ISEFs. Moreover, who knows that ISEFs may, in fact, be communicating. Since these are subtle forms and our knowledge about the behaviour of subtle forms is not known, it may not be possible to know whether ISEFs communicate with each other. But using the logic of these being in jelly-like mass they are all connected and maybe insulated but communications may be happening with a breach of insulation between them*

Next unanswered question: It tells about ISEF entering the living things when fertilization takes place in living females (be it human or non-human)—is fertilization caused by the entry of ISEF into the body or is independent of it i.e., do ISEFs enter after fertilization or their entry is the cause of fertilization?---***This indeed is a question warranting detailed and deep research.***

Philosophically speaking it is said that life enters the womb only when a soul enters the embryo and hence the fertilizing may be caused by the entry of the soul which in our theory is the ISEF. ISEF's transformation to SELF is the cause of fertilization and in manifesting a live energy entity. Medically speaking how and when does fertilization happens in humans is explained in an article written by Zawn Villines (2020) and explained by Valinda Riggins Nwadike, MD. The author describes the fertilization process as under:

"Getting pregnant may seem like a rather mystical process. You may wonder how long it takes to actually conceive after having sex. -- The short answer is that the egg and sperm can meet within minutes to up to 12 hours after ejaculation. ***But the fertilization occurs when the egg and sperm meet in the*** *fallopian tube. In order for this to happen, a woman must be in her fertile window. This means that she's nearing or has reached ovulation — the moment each menstrual cycle when an egg gets released from the ovary.*

An egg can only be fertilized between 12 and 24 hours from when it is released. After that, it starts to break down, hormones shift, and eventually, a period starts the next cycle.

While it sounds like the chances of catching an egg are pretty slim, consider the numbers. It's estimated ejaculate contains up to 280 million sperm cells. And under ideal conditions, sperm actually live for several days once inside the reproductive tract.

Any unprotected sex you have within about 5 days of ovulation may leave enough sperm waiting and ready to fertilize. In other words, you may conceive after having sex nearly a week before ovulation if healthy sperm are already hanging out at their final destination.

On the flip side, conception can occur very soon after having sex as well. Experts say that the sperm can navigate the uterus and fallopian tubes to reach the egg as soon as 30 minutes after ejaculation."

This would mean that till fertilization happens meeting of sperm and egg is only a chemical action and there is a delay in making it become a biological phenomenon when fertilization happens in the fallopian tube. The writer calls fertilization a mystical process, probably hinting towards life manifestation only by fertilization. Though not explicitly told, even medical thought appears to support that life manifestation happens when fertilization happens and the chemical process of amalgamation of sperm and egg becomes a biological process. Thus, we may not be wrong in theorizing that the transformation of ISEF into SLEF happens with fertilization and the transformation may be the causal factor for fertilization. We took a specific example of humans but maybe it is true for all living species which manifest with ISEF transformation into SLEF

Last unanswered question: Energy Survival Theory is silent about the conscious experience which happens at the time of death either by the then live SLEF or its unique ISEF.

Answer to this last point led me to research in detail about the death experience which is discussed in detail in my recently published book, "What happens When and After We Die". The book covers all aspects of death, starting from death's definition to the meaning of death, the death experience, and what is life after death.

The answer to the last question is discussed in details in the following paragraphs:

Conscious experience which happens at the time of death

How does a person feel at the time of death? Is the feeling the same for all living entities (SLEFs of all living species-human as well as non-human) at the time of death or different live entities have different feelings? Do humans feel differently than the other living entities? Do all humans have the same feeling at the time of death or different humans experience death in different ways? These are the questions for which we do not have answers because as stated earlier also because the experiencer cannot describe their experiences because the ticket is one way.

In the following paragraphs, we will explore this aspect of human experience, details of which are still not known scientifically. Maybe the other living non-human species may be undergoing a similar death experience.

What exactly is the feeling of the person when he is dying, can at best be a matter of imagination. We shall, all, undergo that experience one day and we do not know whether it will be identical with the experiences of others or will it be a unique tailor-made for each person distinct from others. Imaginations can stretch to any limits and we can associate several feelings to the dying person. But what exactly is going in a person's mind, what his consciousness is experiencing while he is dying is not known. The reason is obvious, there is an impasse because the person experiencing death cannot come back and narrate the incident. Well, then, is there no way that we could learn what is happening when one is dying?? The experiencer of death cannot come back and narrate the experience—hence we reach an impasse!!

The human mind is innovative and finds out way out of all impasse.

Just think, how could brain research brain—it was an impasse! –how could brain research itself?

But the human brain overcame the impasse and today we know a lot about the brains- of humans as well as of other species. We have learned a lot about brain intricacies; however, it is also true that we are yet to know a lot about the brain. A large portion is still unexplored. But whatever we learned is so fascinating that we are just awestruck. If you ask me what is the most wonderful complex machine on earth it is the human brain!!

The human brain research took clues from the study of brains of people having some impairment resulting in their abnormal behaviour and when the brain circuitry was compared with that of a normal person, we could deduce the cause of abnormal behaviour and, thus, learned what portion of the brain does what. The details of this learning journey are well brought out in the book by Ramachandran V S (2010) in his book, "Tell-Tale Brain".

Maybe we could take a clue from above and try to learn what is happening when life is getting impaired as was brain researched when the brain was impaired. The human mind of a person whose life is getting impaired would be experiencing events that will never be the same for a person leading a healthy life. We can certainly extract the experience from the person who has not died but his life was impaired when he was on the verge of death.

There are many Near-death Experiences (NDEs) reported across the globe. A study of those experiences may point to some common factors which may lead us to what a person experiences when he is dying.

Let us look at some NDEs as available in the literature and then compare analyze them and see if there is some commonality between the reported near-death experiences.

Deepak Chopra (2006) talks about Near Death Experiences as follows:

NDE—In a 1991 Gallup poll, 13 million Americans, roughly 5% of the population, reported that they had near-death experiences.

Near-death is a momentary brush with another reality, or so it may seem to those who report the experience.

A person is lying in the emergency room or intensive care unit. His heart stops, and for all intents and purposes, death ensues. Yet some of these patients, typically those who suffered cardiac arrest, can be resuscitated. When they are, nearly 20 % report at least one of the familiar symptoms of NDE (as near-death experience is abbreviated in the medical literature) ---leaving their bodies, looking down and seeing themselves on the operating table, watching medical procedures being performed as doctors tried to restart their hearts. (pp37)

The author describes the sensations and feelings of the persons who were dying but were resuscitated and when they came back; they described their experience as "***finding themselves in a tunnel, going towards a bright light, feeling the presence of a higher power, hearing or seeing loved ones beckoning them on.***"

Deepak Chopra in the same book is describing the experience of a person who came back after NDE in great details- let us go through this detailed experience cited in his book:

One person who reported his near-death experience in great detail came close to describing ***eternity.*** *The account, now famous in near-death literature, comes from an artist named Mellen-Thomas Benedict, who died of a brain tumour in 1982. That he could be dead for an hour and a half, only to return to life, is not credible by Western standards.*

He found himself out of the body, aware that his corpse was lying in bed. His perception was greatly expanded---he could see over, around, and under his house---and he sensed that he was enveloped in darkness, ***but soon a brilliant light became evident. He moved toward it, aware that if he entered the light, he would be dead.***

At this point, Benedict made a startling decision. He asked for the experience to stop, and it did. Benedict called a halt so that he could talk to the light. As he did so, it continually changed shapes, sometimes resembling Jesus or Budhha, other times turning into a complex pattern like a mandala or archetypal images and signs, as he puts it. ***The light told him (or to be precise, transferred information to his mind) that a dying person is given a "feedback loop" of images that fits their belief system. Being a loop, the dying person can enter into the experience and shape it, as Benedict found***

himself doing. (The light explained that he was a rare case: most people move ahead without question.)

Next Benedict became aware that what he was actually seeing was the Higher Self Matrix, which he describes as a "mandala of human souls"; that is, a cosmic pattern of consciousness. Each person, he realized, has a higher Self that serves as an oversoul and also as a conduit back to the source.

Getting at the matrix of souls, Benedict became aware they were all connected; humanity formed one being; each of us is an aspect of wholeness. He was drawn into the matrix, which he describes as ineffably beautiful. It radiated a healing, generative love that overwhelmed him. The light conveyed to him that the soul matrix formed a subtle energy level that girded the earth and bound people together.

Benedict was experiencing profound ecstasy as he was absorbed deeper into the light, reaching another realm that was subtler but also much very vast. ***He beheld an "enormous stream of light, vast and full, deep in the heart of life." When he asked what it was, the light told him it was the river of life and that he should drink from it to his heart's content.***

Fuelled by limitless curiosity, he now asked to reveal the entire universe to him "beyond all human illusion". ***He was told to ride the stream of life, and as he did, he passed through the tunnel hearing "soft sonic booms" on the way****. His speed accelerated beyond the speed of light as he left the solar system and passed through the heart of the galaxy and became aware of many worlds and many life forms, all in a dizzying rush. At this point, Benedict made a critical discovery that what appeared to be a journey through space was in fact the expansion of his own consciousness. The appearance of galaxies and star clusters racing past was his own consciousness streaming past one boundary of space-time after another.*

Benedict describes entire galaxies disappearing into a point, of all life forms making their presence known, of a second light that contains every vibration in the universe. Benedict was actually witnessing the operation of consciousness itself. Benedict finds his own language for this stage saying that he was interfacing with the hologram of the universe.

Passing into the second light, he experienced a profound shift into silence and utter stillness. It came to him that he could see to infinity. He was in the void, or pre-creation as he calls it, and his consciousness was limitless. He was in contact with the absolute, which wasn't a religious experience but one of unbounded awareness. He perceived all of creation generating itself without beginning or end. Instead of one "Big Bang", a singular event that created the universe, Benedict perceived millions of Big Bangs constantly generating new universes. Since he was beyond time, this was happening simultaneously in all dimensions.

After reaching this cosmic epiphany, Benedict's journey reversed itself step-by-step, and he woke up in his bed at home with the unshakable realization, now so familiar in the NDE literature, that death was an illusion.

Benedict assumed that his return to earth would be as a baby, in a new reincarnation. When he opened his eyes, however, he still had the same body, one that had been dead for over an hour according to the hospice worker who was present (there was no monitoring machinery or doctor). The hospice worker, who had been crying over him, assured Benedict that he had shown every sign of being dead, including a growing cold stiffness in his body. An amplified telescope showed no heartbeat. (in and of itself this claim is medically so outrageous that it would lead a skeptic to discount every other part of Benedict's story)

Although severely disoriented at first, Benedict felt better than he had in his life. It took him three months to chance a new brain scan, being nervous about his tumour—but it proved to be great news. All traces of malignancy were gone, which his oncologist explained as a spontaneous remission, a rare example of a malignancy disappearing on its own. This sidesteps the issue that remissions through death are not found in medical literature, and remissions of advanced brain tumours, so far as I know, are the rarest of occasions.

Benedict's observation *"Getting at the matrix of souls, Benedict became aware they were all connected; humanity formed one being; each of us is an aspect of the wholeness."* ***goes on to confirm the structural aspects of the Extended Energy Survival theory that ISEF and SLEF are embedded in jelly-like cobweb structures where all entities are connected.***

The above experience is a vivid explanation given by the person who apparently was experiencing death. The experience appears to be out of our world. One fact which is common with the previous experience mentioned by Deepak Chopra ***was experiencing a bright light at the start of the experience and passing through a tunnel.***

All NDEs talk about experiencing a strong white light almost blinding their observation when they are transcending to meet death. The scientific mind would like to describe these as morbid thoughts projected by the mind undergoing trauma and pain.

Could this be morbidity at work because the person had come out of trauma or was it that he was really experiencing death, is not known? We shall take up this question later, first let us observe another NDE incident, this time from the book of Erica Simons:

An experience of a person who "came back"

Kenneth G. was successfully resuscitated from death due to a heart attack. But he was not happy to be "back" and told those around him, "when I go again, please leave me alone". In an interview, he described vividly the overwhelming powerful experience that befell him during the minutes he was dead.

I found myself in the most enchanting place you could ever visit. The beauty was beyond anything that I had ever seen before in my life. It was so luxuriant that there is absolutely no way to express to you the intense enjoyment I felt at that place. I discovered myself drifting down to a huge valley. It sloped downward from low, gentle rolling hills. There were miles upon miles of ...flat rolling plains. I was flowing down very slowly like a man with a parachute. I drifted out of the sky and landed softly in a field of grass that came up to my waist. It was a delightful experience. Then I saw this meadow went on forever. I saw dense forests in the far distance...The only word I seem to be able to use to talk about that place is beautiful...As I stood there in the middle of the lush green field, I could see animals, flowers, and trees. It was flowers that I especially liked. I'd never before seen anything like the profusion of growing beautiful plants and flowers in this place.

For a while I stood in the grass, listening to the gentle rustle of grass being blown by a gentle breeze. That, for a while, was the only sound. Then I heard a voice calling me. It was so faint that I just felt that someone is trying to talk to me. It got a little louder. I did not see the person calling me but I recognize the owner of the voice. It was my father, who had died some ten years ago. What is he doing here? The voice kept telling me "Kenneth, don't be afraid. Do not worry, I have come to help you with your journey. Don't be afraid of this. I have helped others.

Then some joyous laughter rolled across the meadow and caught my eyes. I looked across the grass and up the slight curvature of the hill in the distance. There in a broad expanse that was separated from the trees, I saw children playing in the amusement park. They looked very familiar.... The park was like the one that I remembered as a child— Steeplechase Park in Coney Island...But all my old playmates were there, just like what they were sixty years ago...None of them noticed me; they continued to play in the amusement park as we had done half a century ago...I was a little boy again, reliving youth...God it was beautiful!

The incidents elaborate on the death experience as a pleasant experience and also takes on the pleasant surprise of seeing dead near ones in a delightful environment.

Taylor Steve (2018) talks about transformation through dying: *Typically, near-death experiences begin with a feeling of separation from the body (or out-of-body experience), sometimes with a humming or whistling sound. Then there is usually a journey through a dark passage or tunnel towards a place of light. There is a feeling of serenity and intense well-being, a sense of calmness and wholeness, which is often so pleasant that some people are reluctant to return to their bodies, and even feel disappointed when they regain consciousness. Often people meet deceased relatives or beings of light. In a smaller proportion of cases, there is a "life review," in which the significant events of a person's life are replayed.*

The feeling of separation from body signifies that SLEF transformation to ISEF has commenced with a humming or whistling sound. In a way, the experience supports the Extended Energy Survival Theory.

Taylor discounts the Hallucinations as an explanation for this experience because NDEs feel much more real. There is also a sense of connectedness or unity. The sense of being a separate entity, enclosed within our own mental space, is replaced by a sense of being part of an interconnected network of beings, of sharing identity with other people--- ***again we get a similar view of the structure of ISEF and SLEF being embedded in Jelly, interconnected with each other as per the Extended Energy Survival Theory.***

Near-death experiences are controversial because it is difficult to explain them in neurological terms. Many suggestions have been made—for example, that they are caused by cerebral anoxia, by undetected brain activity, or the release of "psychedelic chemicals" like DMT or ketamine in the brain when a person is close to death.

Erica Simon's book goes beyond the above neurological explanation and gives logical reasons against the above neurological explanation. She brings out detailed research and analysis of NDEs in her book citing the work of a parapsychologist Dr. Karlis Osis deeply engaged in NDEs:

Parapsychologist Dr. Karlis Osis knows more about death visions than anyone else in the world. Since 1960 he has investigated over one hundred thousand deaths and revealed the results in his two books-Deathbed observations by Physicians and Nurses (1961) and At the Hour of death (1977). As the title of first suggests, his information was gathered directly from doctors and Nurses, an ideal source because of the number of deaths they witness, and the fact that their medical training requires them to observe and record patient's reactions. The view that no one has ever "come back" to tell us about death is an extremely popular one- but it is also untrue. The experiences come from the world beyond death. They happened to people who were technically dead—whose hearts had stopped beating, whose lungs had ceased to function, whose blood pressure had dropped so low that it was unreadable, whose pupils had dilated, whose body temperatures had begun to sink. They are "experiences "in the sense that they are detailed accounts of what people say happened to them between the time their bodies died and the time they were resuscitated.

According to the information his medical sources provided, only about ten percent of those who die are conscious shortly before death, and thus, able to report deathbed events. Of this group, how many undergo the kinds of experiences discussed above?? Unfortunately,

Osis's research does not directly answer this question, but a careful examination of his statistics suggests that from one-half to two-thirds of conscious dying patients have these experiences! Such frequencies are unique to the dying, for only 10-17 percent of people in normal health ever have hallucinations of any kind! What exactly happens to the dying? – Three things: apparitional visits from dead loved ones, glimpses of the "next world" and medically inexplicable moods of elation. (pp99).

The testimony of those who returned from death reveals two quite different things that happen when that awesome boundary is crossed. Some report that they lacked any trace of consciousness and so experienced nothing but a "blank", the rest report extremely vivid experiences. Why these variations occur we do not yet know. The stories of those who have travelled beyond life and returned to living describe their most mysterious journeys –these actually resemble those of early geographical explorers in the ancient world. Reports that conscious existence continues after clinical death are not accepted by contemporary medicine and science, and people describing such incidences are assumed to be suffering from hallucinations caused by the trauma of temporary death. But in opposition to this modern view of death is a very ancient human tradition that holds that the death of the body does not bring one's personal existence to an end.

The above paragraph answers one question as to whether different people have the same experience while dying or their experiences are different. Unlike previous narrations where it was said that all experience "A light" and a "tunnel"; here description is given of happiness while dying as there happens a meeting with dead near ones and an experience of beautiful place (we may give it a name as Heaven).

We had left one question to be taken up subsequently which was- Could these death experiences be a creation of mind due to morbidity caused by the death trauma and the pain the person was feeling when moving towards death.

The above book takes on the debate whether the visions and experiences narrated in NDEs are due to morbid condition of the brain:

Are the death visions, exalted moods, and reported death experiences by the dying real, or are they hallucinations?

If you are suffering from 'Cerebral Anoxia' your brain is not getting enough oxygen to operate normally. Cerebral Anoxia was often mentioned by doctors and nurses as one of the likeliest explanations for deathbed visions. To see whether this was the real cause, Osis separated all of the dying people who had hand visions into two groups: those who, in the opinion of doctors and nurses, were suffering from cerebral anoxia, and those who weren't. It turned out that anoxia made no difference. The visions of the dying patients with cerebral anoxia were indistinguishable from those of other patients.

Cerebral Anoxia could not, therefore, be the cause of these experiences.

Deathbed visions cannot be explained by the medical condition of the dying person, nor by the state of his mind, nor by religious or cultural background. How, then, can we explain them?

The only remaining possibility is that these are genuine psyche experiences. Being close to death can apparently create an altered state of consciousness which captures the experience and makes it deeply etched in memory and is reported in detail when a person returns back from the threshold of death.

If we can accept these experiences as glimpses into the beyond death- and Osis's research strongly suggests that we have no alternative—

then we are ready to venture further into this astounding world. (pp94,99)

Two things emerge from Dr. Osis's research and analysis

The NDE phenomena are not due to hallucination experienced by the brain due to lack of oxygen in the brain (*Cerebral Anoxia)* but are real happenings and can be considered as genuine experiences while we transcend from life towards death and beyond if at all there is life after death.

The mood at the time of death is of happiness due to entering a beautiful environment—his research does not speak of "Bright light" or passing through "Tunnel" but does mention a sense of happiness at the time of "death" and reaching a joyous beautiful environment.

The NDE incidents cited are in agreement on the above two points and we are led to believe that death is not traumatic to the person who is dying. It may be a traumatic experience to the near dear ones whom the departing person is leaving behind in our world and they will feel the pain and undergo bereavement but the person meeting death is experiencing joy and happiness when he is transcending from life to death.

Siofra Brenin (2016) in an article gives a vivid account of feelings of persons who experienced death in their NDEs:

Barabra describes her NDE –I "died three times after separate surgeries, wherein my heart and respiration slow to a stop within minutes. Although I could hear perfectly (the beeping of the monitor as I flatlined, the code of the PA, the squeak-squeak of the crash-cart wheel, everyone talking at once), I had no other sensation. As I was sinking into unconsciousness, I felt very cool, relaxed, no need to breathe, no cause of alarm, no pain of any kind, totally peaceful. Everything grew dark around the edges until there was only blackness

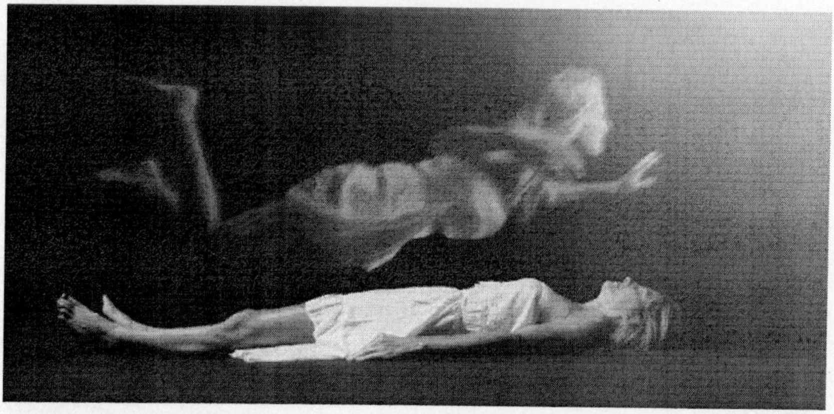

The above is an imaginary picture of an NDE, where the person experiences floating out of the body and witnessing her own physical body from outside

The feelings of the dying person Barbara who came back to life, again, explains it to be joyful and not to be dreaded or of pain. The fact that she was hearing the sounds when consciousness was fading is indicative of confirming Indian faith that sound is the last sense to leave the body.

Another person Scott had a very brief encounter with death

Three years ago, I had some heart issues and my doctor sent me home wearing something called a "Life Vest" – essentially a bunch of monitors and an external defibrillator. A week or so later I had a cardiac arrest. The monitors shoed as flatlining... but the vets did it and resuscitated me. The process of 'dying" was remarkably peaceful... I have no recollection. When I eventually die on a more permanent basis, I can hope it's as peaceful as the first time.

Even the brief glimpse of death was peaceful and comforting to the extent that he wishes that when he eventually meats death, he should have the same feelings as he had during that short encounter.

Another death experience:

Dea died twice in September 26.2009. My first thought after I saw a gorgeous white light at the top of the mountain in front of me was, "Oh my God. I am dead!" There were many other people walking up the mountain towards the light. But I was furious. All I could think about was how I had been to the emergency room so many times and had been blown off and "now I am dead." I did not look down at my own body, unfortunately, but the other dead people just l looked like regular people. I felt no pain, I was just angry. After a few minutes, my cousin sort of popped right in front of me and told me, "Deanne, go back" I haven't been called Deanne since I was a kid and she was one of the people who knew me as "Deanne". When I turned around to see what she meant by "back" I was slammed into my bed at the hospital with seven doctors and nurses yelling at me, "stay with us". Pain returned. I was in shock. I will never forget my two and half minutes being dead.

The death experience makes the person lose the feeling of pain and shock and the return from death brings back these feelings. The feeling of anger for being in the hospital frequently lingers on during death and the feeling stayed on death. Like other death experiences, Dea does experience "bright light" and as per her experiences all recently dead have to walk towards the "bright light", meaning thereby that all people experience the "bright light"—this has been described by many experiencers of death. She experienced union with a deceased relative, which is also experienced by many people who have come back from death in NDEs.

I end up NDE aspects with the narration of a death experience in which a person feels that there is no afterlife.

"Emmanuel mentions- a few years ago, I had a severe case of undiagnosed pneumonia which had gone untreated for many weeks, eventually things went so bad that I landed up in the intensive care unit. My heart was starting to fail, I could hardly speak. There was

nothing exciting about what was coming. In fact. it wasn't anything. No light, no hope, nothing. Only darkness and loneliness.

There was no pain, just darkness, extreme vulnerability, extreme fragility, and nothing. If someone, something was left of me, it was a silent, naked, compassionate, honest, sad, and helpless being of undetermined age, social status, or civilization, who could look at its/ his/ her imminent end and nobody being of help or even to come through (not that anyone mattered anymore, anyway). It wasn't even revolting or scary, just infinite sadness and nothingness. After a while life came back to me and then it was another story entirely.

Based on this experience, I am inclined to feel that there is nothing after our life."

Emmanuel recounts that there was no feeling experienced when he had transcended to death, only a vacuum and infinite nothingness.

Summarizing the death experience narrative, I wish to first state that there are no scientific details available as to how a person feels when he is dying. At least I could not come across any literature which brings out the feelings of a dying person in a scientific way. The nearest we could approach death scientifically was defining death clinically, which states that with the death of the brain stem, a person cannot be revived to consciousness and he loses consciousness permanently and meets death and is declared to be dead. Why do we "declare" why don't we "diagnose"!!

Rooper Allan (2014) gives some reasoning for this

"Brain Stem death is a firm, unambiguous, and operationally solid determination, an absolute point of no return for the brain. Any two competent neurologists or neurosurgeons who examine a braindead patient will come to the same conclusion, the brain will never recover, and all the king's horses and men can't do a damn thing about it.

The problem is the word dead. It muddies the important issue, as does the diagnosis. Brain death is not a diagnosis—a word that suggests probability—but rather a determination. A diagnosis raises the spectre of false positives, of fallibility, of someone being buried alive."

Thus, we see that death is not diagnosed because diagnosis leaves a trace of doubt and does not state deterministically that person is dead so doctors declare the death- which means a certainty that person cannot be resuscitated and cannot come back to life.

In scientific terms, consciousness is permanently gone.

We know the meaning of death but to arrive at the dying experience, we can logically arrive at the death experience only by analyzing a vast number of near-death experience (NDE) cases. The observational theory will not be far from the truth, only causal aspects of the theory will not be known and scientific research must one day find out the causal aspects.

Before we zero down on the exact feelings of death experience a person has while undergoing NDE, I want to reassert that the feelings do not arise out of the hallucination or brain condition of the person in a traumatic condition. We have already discussed this in detail and seen reasonings on this in previous paragraphs. The reasons given for the NDEs being real death experiences are sound and we must, therefore, accept that the feelings of a dying person are correctly reflected in NDE incidents.

We shall have a brief relook into the feelings reported by several experiencers of NDEs and shall then summarize what a person feels when dying. But before we attempt that, I wish you to take a look at what a researcher has to say in this regard:

Deepak Chopra (2006) mentions an American survey that found that 5% of the population experienced NDE. 20% of the people undergoing cardiac arrest report NDE. They experience ***finding themselves in a tunnel, going towards a bright light, feeling the presence of a higher power, hearing or seeing loved ones beckoning them on."***

Other NDEs mention the appearance of ***a brilliant light coming from the other side of the tunnel in which they move at the time of death. The light conveys to the dying that the soul matrix formed a subtle energy level that girded the earth and bound people together.***

This is what my Extended Energy Survival Theory maintains that the souls are nothing but subtle energies which I call ISEFs

The experience of Kenneth G, described by Erica Simons, was so pleasant that he expressed anguish on being resuscitated to life. He experienced a lush green meadow and was met by his dead cousin. The beauty of the valley was so impressive that he had never witnessed it in his lifetime. The environment was joyously filled with the laughter of discarnate entities and he liked being a part of it.

Taylor Steve summarizes the Experience of death in the following manner: The near-death experiences begin with a feeling of separation from the body, sometimes with a humming or whistling sound. Then there is usually a journey through a dark passage or tunnel towards a place of light. There is a feeling of serenity and intense well-being, a sense of calmness and wholeness, which is often so pleasant that some people are reluctant to return to their bodies, and even feel disappointed when they regain consciousness.

Dr. Karlis Osis an authority on NDEs had been investigating NDE cases since 1960 and had a first-hand account of the cases from patients and attending doctors and nurses. He summarizes the death experiences as--- ***What exactly happens to the dying? - medically inexplicable moods of elation. The testimony of those who returned from death reveals two quite different things that happen when that awesome boundary is crossed. Some report that they lacked any***

trace of consciousness and so experienced nothing but a "blank", the rest report extremely vivid experiences as described above.

Siofra Brenin (2016) in an article gives a vivid account of feelings of persons who experienced death in their NDEs: *Barabara felt "as I was sinking into unconsciousness, I felt very cool, relaxed, no need to breathe, no cause of alarm, no pain of any kind, totally peaceful. Everything grew dark around the edges until there was only blackness. She was* joyful and not dreaded or no feeling of pain.

Dea felt death experience as "I saw a gorgeous white light at the top of the mountain in front of me. There were many other people walking up the mountain towards the light. I felt no pain, I was just angry.

Emmanuel mentions about death experience as "There was nothing exciting in what was coming. In fact. it wasn't anything. No light, no hope, nothing. Only darkness and loneliness. There was no pain, just darkness, extreme vulnerability, extreme fragility, and nothing. If someone, something was left of me, it was silent, naked, compassionate, honest, sad, and helpless. It wasn't even revolting or scary, just infinite sadness and nothingness."

The above paragraphs give summaries of various NDEs where the persons undergo death experiences. These observational experiences when condensed can lead us to a theory about death experience. The Observational Theory, based on real experiences of people who faced death but came back to narrate the experience will fall short of scientific theory but it cannot be brushed aside as mere nonsense. NDEs, as we saw, cannot be brain conditions or hallucinations because of the reasons discussed in the above paragraphs so these must be real and factual experiences when death is taking a person in its fold.

The condensing of all the above experiences leads us to include a theory describing the death experience into the Extended Energy Survival Theory. Here it goes:

When a person, the SLEF in current life is dying,. it experiences a feeling of separation from the physical body, sometimes with a humming or whistling sound. There is a feeling of serenity and intense well-being, a sense of calmness and wholeness, which is often so pleasant that some manifested SLEFs are reluctant to return to their bodies, and even feel disappointed when they regain consciousness. Then a total blackout ensues temporarily and then some SLEFs experience a feeling of passing through a tunnel and approaching a very bright shining light. The bright light, in rare situations, communicates and if the dying SLEF expresses a desire to stop entering the light, he could be allowed to return back to the world and an NDE manifests.

In other instances, SLEFs do not see a tunnel or bright white light but straight away arrive at the next stage which puts them in an environment that is beyond worldly explanation; the best explanation is a happy blissful environment. To some it is passing through lush green meadows, tall grass fluttering with the breeze, and delightful colourful flowers blossoming all around. At this stage, SLEFs experience a meeting with their dear ones who had died. Apparitional visits from dead loved ones, glimpses of the "next world" and medically inexplicable moods of elation manifest. The testimony of those who returned from death reveals two quite different things happen when that awesome boundary is crossed. Some report that they lacked any trace of consciousness and so experienced nothing but a "blank", the rest report extremely vivid experiences as described above.

The above is the derivation of the death experience from several NDEs and captures the most probable feelings of a person (SLEF in our theory) who is in the process of dying.

Linking it to our Extended Energy Survival theory, the SLEF at its last stage (that of death) before it gets transformed to its unique ISEF undergoes above experiences and a common experience is of passing through a tunnel from whose opposite end a bright light is approaching and the overall experience is not traumatic but blissful. The transformation could be accompanied by humming or whistling sound as experienced by some experiencer of NDE.

The theory though based on the scientific base of Energy theory is still not a scientific theory. In fact, the subject "death and afterlife" could not get researched the way other parapsychological fields were investigated through rigorous laboratory experimental testing because experiments are not possible for obvious reasons.

The credibility of mediums who claimed to possess the capability of calling spirits and talking to them was dimmed when famous mediums were found using fraudulent measures in their seances.

It is, indeed, a fact that trickery was proved in many so-called paranormal incidents. The "Mediums" were using fraudulent methods to prove anomalous through trickery just to gain popularity, fame, and for making fortunes. Hansen (2001) gives details of many seemingly credible paranormal events, which came crashing down after trickery was proved. One such event was of Fox sisters, which had a very prominent impact on people, till trickery was admitted. Hansen has summarized various famous trickeries in his paper.

Caroline Watt has made subtle remarks on the above issues of deception and fraud in mediums and survival research: “For over 150 years, psychical researchers and parapsychologists have investigated whether physical and mental mediumship provide any evidence for life after death. Early work into table-turning, spirit rapping, and materialization often revealed evidence of fraud, trickery, and self-deception. Although some studies with renowned mental mediums such as Leonara Piper and Eileen Garret convinced even some skeptical researchers that they possessed psychic abilities, arguments over whether this evidence signified paranormal communication with the deceased or with the living reached a stalemate.

More controlled studies that prevented sources of error or bias have generally not yielded evidence of the afterlife. However, regardless of the position, one takes on the survival question, research into mediumship and reincarnation has undoubtedly revealed a great deal about the psychology of deception, the unreality of eyewitness testimony, and the challenges of designing a methodically sound investigation."

Currently, we find ourselves at crossroads and do not have any evidence for or against life after death. But should we leave the issue unresolved or take some steps to reach some evidence to prove /disprove the theories of life after death?

I think, as stated for other fields of Parapsychology, the answer lies in pursuing Causal "Life After Death" Research which is going to be the most difficult compared to other Parapsychological fields. But we must make a beginning by finding some approach that could take us to the causal research.

In the next paragraphs, we shall try to discover whether there could be some approach that could lead us in the direction of Causal "Life After Death" Research.

Scientific research has still not begun for Survival after death as was done for other psi fields for which laboratory experimentations and statistical analyses could be undertaken. What is preventing Causal Survival Research—what are the impediments, even though discussed in the previous chapter we shall once again recall these as these will lay a foundation for our discussions on Causal aspects of Survival Research.

Naresh Kumar (2020) explains this in his paper, “Life after death—Contemporary theories and Beyond”:

Impediments pertaining to Causal Survival Research

Besides the frauds, another aspect that proved a major stumbling block to causal Survival Research is the primitive stage in which this research finds itself. The Survival Research so far confines to only philosophical thinking --- maybe the causal research is not possible because the ticket is one way-you die, but you cannot come back to tell what happened to you when you died. In fact, an attempt has not been made towards causal survival research because the phenomena are not observable like other aspects of Parapsychology where there were people who could relate and explain their paranormal experiences of Telepathy. Clairvoyance/ Remote viewing, Precognition, or Psychokinesis. In the case of survival research, this is not possible because the person experiencing death cannot explain the phenomenon so we cannot have a first-hand account of what happens after death. This is the major hurdle towards Causal Survival Research.

Fear of death may be another factor that may be preventing us to probe this area causally. The after-death research may be a dreaded area to probe in. ignorance breeds fear and since we are totally ignorant about what happens when and after we die and the fear of death is at the forefront when we talk about researching life after death. People simply do not want to talk about it, not to talk about researching it. To elaborate on this point, I recall the incident of Gaurav Tiwari.

In India, the founder of the Indian Paranormal Society---Mr. Gaurav Tiwari, who was actively involved in the research on Survival after death, met mysterious death at the age of 31, and, to date, the mystery of his death is not solved. A faint black ring was found around his neck--- what caused this, could not be established. Before his death, he had expressed his feelings that negative powers are pulling him towards them!!"

There is an impasse reached because to explain what happens after we die and if we die, we cannot come back and tell our experiences.

This impasse is the greatest hurdle as we are not getting an account of what we experience unlike other aspects of Parapsychological fields of research. This reason alone prevented experimental research In Survival Research. In other fields viz telepathy/ remote viewing, psychokinesis we could go in for experimental research in the laboratory because the experience could be explained by the experiencer but in the case of Survival Research, we have reached the impasse because the experiencer cannot explain the experience of death.

But still, we have to find a way:

Trending towards Causal Survival Research

To start with we could look up the work done by Frederick Myers who initiated survival research in 1882 by starting the Society for Psychic Research in the UK. There is a book published posthumously and there are, presumably, documented posthumous messages from Frederick Myers to work on. The relevance of his work to current researchers is well brought out by Mark B Ryan in his paper, "The Resurrection of Frederic Myers" While the work of Frederic Myers is still relevant to the question of life after death, it is more intriguing to notice his efforts of communicating even after his death. He was so dedicated that it is evidenced that his work continued even after his death(in 1901) and that he continued to communicate till 1933 to psychics around the world in his own style by giving fragmented pieces of information which did not make any sense to the receiver but when pooled at SPR as per Myers instructions, fitted like a jigsaw puzzle and brought forth his thoughts comprehensively. These aspects are well covered in a book by Erica Simon, (2006)

The pooled information received from discarnate Frederic Myers by different mediums gives details about seven stages after death. The details are covered in a paper entitled "Frederic Myers Afterlife

Communication" which is an excerpt from the book by a lawyer Victor Zammit The paper gives details as hereunder:

"The following is a description of these stages as communicated by discarnate Myer (after death messages from Myer)- The section on the Myers correspondences are reprinted by permission from Victor Zammit:

- ***Stage one*** after death is, of course, the Earth realm. As soon as the Earth experience has been thoroughly comprehended - either through reincarnation or through the exchange of experience with others on other realms - the candidate may proceed to realms beyond the reach of the Earth mind. After death, a person enters Stage two, the Intermediate Realm.
- ***Stage Two-*** Upon death, most people go through a heavenly process before entering into heaven. Evil people, instead of experiencing the tunnel and bright light upon death, are sent through what Sylvia calls the "Left Door" and enter into an abyss of empty, joyless, nothingness for a brief period of time. After they have reflected upon their actions, they are reincarnated back to Earth. People who commit suicide are sent to a place Sylvia calls the "Holding Place." Here they must make a choice to either proceed through the "Left Door" or embrace God and move on to the Light. People in the Holding Place shuffle slowly around in despair in a gray fog with their heads down until they make their decision. According to Sylvia, this is purgatory.
- ***Stage three***--After Stage two, a person enters a more stable world called "the realm of illusion". This is a dimension where things may be created with the mind and shaped by the direct action of the imagination. Though a person may linger in this stage for generations, an eventual decision must be made. The individual either returns to Earth or

progresses to Stage four. Before leaving, however, the more enterprising souls may have an opportunity to experience one of the great wonders of this realm of consciousness - a tour through some section of "The Great Memory." Just as on Earth, one may go to a library and see newsreels of important Earth events of history. So, in Stage three, one may witness any event that has occurred from the beginning of the human experience. Everything that has ever happened has been recorded by cosmic memory.

Spiritualists call this realm "the second heaven." Most people who die initially find themselves in the second heaven or intermediate astral realms. Viewed as a sort of resting point on the way from Earth to the more ratified upper dimensions, it is a thought-created universe that closely resembles an idealized Earth. Its inhabitants seem to live in physical bodies, wear clothes, and so forth - but of an etheric kind that would be invisible on Earth. Most attempts to communicate from heaven stem from here; but because its inhabitants are as yet unfamiliar with the afterlife, these communications can be confusing or wrong.

- ***Stage four***- an indescribably lovely existence, is called "the realm of colour." Here one must leave behind all rigid intellectual structures and dogmas, be they scientific, religious, or philosophical. An infinite variety of new sounds, colours, and feelings are experienced here and souls find much wider freedom to function with more highly energized intellect and spirit. *Since Myers had not progressed beyond the fourth realm at the time of his communication, his reports of the higher levels of consciousness beyond this are less detailed and more speculative. He seems to have picked up enough hearsay, however, to outline with some confidence the general nature of the further advance.*

If on the fourth realm, the soul becomes free from the Earth pull, the soul is qualified to experience cosmic ranges beyond Earth's confines. One of these ranges is the next realm, "***the realm of flame.***"

- ***Fifth stage***-In the fifth realm, the "***realm of flame,***" one acquires a body of flame, enabling him to tour the stellar universe without being harmed by its temperatures and turbulence and to return with a fuller experience of these cosmic reaches.

  This realm corresponds to the spiritualist's "fourth heaven." In the fourth heaven, which some refer to as the mental and causal realms, most of the trappings of materialism have gone. It is here that selfless individuals work together to bring spiritual enlightenment to the lower slopes of heaven and to Earth. Supposedly all great inventions, religious and moral progressions, spiritual leadership, and so on, come from here, inspired by beings who were once on Earth but have had the opportunity to increase their talents in the afterlife.

  A few rebirths to Earth do take place from this higher realm. Great teachers are sent back for special reasons. Spirit guides who talk through mediums are often in this realm as well, bringing their enhanced knowledge to Earth.
- ***Sixth Stage***-The sixth realm is called by Myers, the "***realm of light.***" Individuals in this realm are matured spirits, having lived through, with conscious comprehension, all the aspects of the created universe. They are capable of living now without form, of existing as white light in the pure thought of the Creator. They have joined the immortals, thus fulfilling their final purpose of the evolution of consciousness.
- ***The seventh stage***, in which the soul enters full partnership with God, is beyond Myers' verbal reach. Myers knew that the levels of consciousness in the upper ranges were beyond the insight of the average Earth dweller except for intuitive flashes. The seventh stage, which Myers called "timelessness," is inhabited by souls with an advanced

> spiritual nature that is so close to the ultimate essence of creativity that no adequate vocabulary has yet evolved to describe them, and hence they are difficult to describe to Earth-level beings.

Since science does not believe in life after death, the above communications from discarnate Frederic Myers have no significance in the realm of science. Maybe if we, the Parapsychologists, take the efforts of passionate Frederic Myers seriously (he had said that he will try to communicate after death); this could be a starting point for Causal Research on life after death. The Parapsychologists must, with help of Physicists and Neuroscientists must try to find ways to explore ways and means to prove/disprove the contents of the messages supposedly coming from Frederic Myers after he died. It is said that for thirty-two years after his death, his messages kept coming so at least we the Parapsychologists must give importance to his persistent efforts for communicating to living human beings and must not brush aside the communication as mere non-sense.

While discussing the impediments on way to causal Survival Research was that unlike other Parapsychological fields where the experiencer was there to explain what he experienced in case of telepathy/clairvoyance/precognition etc. but in the case of survival phenomena the experient of death cannot come and explain what happened when he died and happenings thereafter. This is the reason no laboratory research was done for Survival Research. The experient does not exist to tell the experience but here is the rarest case where the Psychological researcher himself is communicating to us about what happens after we die, but we do ignore it and do not attach any importance to these communications. Is there no credibility in these communications? Remember these stages as being presented in the book were not given exactly in this form but is extracted as a summary from numerous communications received through automatic writings by mediums scattered across the globe. These have not come from one medium so that we could brush it aside as the creation of the mind of that medium. In fact, Frederic Myer when alive had himself experienced ridicule over his communication with spirits through automatic writing. He being an intelligent researcher knew that his messages will reach the same fate so he planned a method of communicating so that the living human intelligentsia does not reject his messages on this ground. He used to communicate through automatic writing only in bits which did not make any sense to the recipient medium but at the end of automatic writing sessions, he used to instruct the medium to forward the message to one source where these were later assembled and these resulted in meaningful messages. The above stages as summarized have emerged from the assembled messages got from many mediums who got these through automatic writing sessions which were dictated by discarnate Frederic Myers. We have no way to explain this happening. We can't even attribute this to the so-called super psi of mediums, since there was not one but many and the messages received by them were meaningless -so even psi or super psi cannot explain these messages coming from a discarnate source.

Another point of thought is that the messages had come clearly till he passed out the fourth stage but he could not communicate exact experiences of the fifth/sixth and seventh stage and he had narrated these while in the fourth stage through the learnings he got from some sources while in the fourth stage. Maybe after reaching the fifth stage there occurred some barriers which prevented communications even with the mediums. The fifth stage onwards may be based on hearsay and not the actual experience but until the 4th stage it is the actual experience and there is strong reason to take those as credible messages and believe them till there is evidence to refute them. Could it be that these messages have truth hidden in them and do we really experience this after we die? I do not know how many of you will buy the logical inference drawn by me. But I am sure that we cannot brush the logic as mere non-sense!!

The impasse of reaching a dead-end for causal survival research, as seen in the above discussions of impediments is the death blocking the experiencer's observations. The impasse or the paradox was similarly faced in brain research as was discussed in foregone passages. I think we should look at this problem with optimism— When Brain could circumvent the impasse and could research itself, which was a matter of impasse like the impasse in life after death where the ticket is one way; there could be a similar way out.

Brain research is happening and the impasse, "brain researching brain", is overcome and we, now, know some aspects of brain functioning, though, a major portion of the brain still remains unexplored and neuroscientists are busy exploring the unknown portion of the brain.

One approach taken in brain research was to understand what caused some brain patients to do weird things—what changes in their brain triggered their weird actions. Comparison of brain patterns of these patients with the brains of normal people led us to an understanding of some parts of the brain. (V S Ramachandran, 2010)

Could we not tow the same line for Survival research? We do have unusual instances (like impaired brains as discussed above) when people have had near-death experiences (NDEs) or when they came back to life after being declared dead (we discussed NDE incidents in paragraphs above). We also have out-of-body experiences. Such real-life events are similar to brain dysfunctional events.

These have similarities with brain malfunctioning which were studied and the studies resulted in brain research--- could we not take a cue from Mr. Ramachandran's approach to brain research and find our own innovative ways to probe death by making use of such unusual death events. Neuroscientists, Medical researchers, and parapsychologists as a team could probably work towards Causal Survival Research by deeply studying such unusual near-death events which might give some clue to life after death, and of course, we have

Frederic Myer's accounts which may get corroborated or disproved. I can point to one corroboration between Myers message and near-death experiences which is narrated in stage 2— "Evil people, instead of experiencing the tunnel and bright light upon death, are sent through the "Left Door" and enter into an abyss of empty, joyless, nothingness for a brief period of time." This tells us that goodpeople experience the tunnel and bright light when they die--- All experiencers of near-death experiences have talked about a bright light in a tunnel.

If stage 2 is true, maybe stage 3 and 4 also must be true!!............

Another possible approach to Causal Survival Research could be through the pursuit of further analysis of the work done by Paranormal Investigators doing work with discarnate spirits.

Sarbajeet Mohanty and Neil D'Silva, (2020) in their book, "Spirits talk to me" give an account of their paranormal investigations of haunted places where the spirits are causing dreaded acts putting people into serious discomforts and agony. The Paranormal team led by Sarbajeet Mohanty using various paranormal gadgets are able to affirm the presence of spirits in the locations where they are troubling people. They used the following instruments in their paranormal investigation:

- PIR sensors (Passive infrared Sensors)-a device with light indicators that light up when there is even a slight movement within its range.
- The EMF pump is an electromagnetic pump. This device contains a magnet that is made to rotate at high speed. The rotation of the magnet produces a magnetic field in the surrounding area. The amplified electromagnetic field helps spirits to make their presence known through changes in the field.
- Full Spectrum GoPro -this is a GoPro Camera that is customized to allow all light frequencies. This enables

inspection of a wider range of the spectrum, including the range in which the parapsychological dimension is believed to exist

- K2 meter—known as Ghost meter, this device is commonly used on paranormal investigations. It measures the electromagnetic force (EMF) in the surroundings. Paranormal science maintains that all entities can alter EMF around them. Hence, any odd fluctuation in K2 meter indicates an unnatural presence. Normally, this meter has five display lights. The first light is always on, as we already have some EMF around us. Known electronic devices in the vicinity can make two or three lights blink but anything beyond will defy scientific explanation and could mean the presence of unseen entities like spirits.
- Equipment PSB-7—it scans FM or AM frequencies at a desirable and controlled speed. It scans frequencies in forward or reverse mode. As it scans, it produces a white noise that the spirit uses to communicate. It is generally used in reverse mode.
- Electronic Detection and Investigation device—This is an all-in-one device that measures electromagnetic field, temperature, auditory disturbances, geometer, and frequencies amongst others.

They could detect the presence of spirits using the above gadgets and could communicate with the spirits to persuade them to stop creating disturbances in the environment. They followed Paranormal protocols and paranormal gadgets while dealing withagitated spirits. There was no physical manifestation of spirits in all investigations but the spirits made their presence known to them by responding to the questions of investigations and their responses were captured by K2 meter and other gadgets.

As per the authors there is no way by which the spirits could appear in their physical form as they may be possessing very feeble energy which prevents them to take physical shape or manifest in some physical form but they do possess the intelligence to communicate and they did communicate in a subtle way and could be got persuaded to leave the haunted spaces and the sufferings of affected human beings were alleviated by the paranormal investigators.

The incidents in the book are real-life incidents and make us aware of many facts about discarnate spirits.

We could work on causal survival research using the knowledge gathered from the paranormal investigations. The authors stopped analysis when their desired results were obtained by freeing the haunted places from clutches of spirits.

We can extend theiranalysis to find the basic reasons which prevent the discarnate from manifesting regularly before live people which makes such incident rare. We can research to find out the conditions which help them to make contact with living people---this approach of causal research may take us towards a better understanding of what happens after we die.

The starting point could be based on the following revelations got from the paranormal investigations:

- The spirits or ghosts exist which is proved beyond doubt by the investigations done by Mohanty and the team
- Since spirits do not possess a physical body, they have difficulty in making their presence visible presumably their inability of assuming physical form is because they possess very feeble energy-so feeble that their movements cannot be felt by humans and we need special equipment to assess their presence, movement and for communicating with them.
- Their presence/movement can be detected by changes in electromagnetic frequency surrounding them.
- The minute EMF generated by them is not possible to detect by normal means, we need special equipment like K2 meter to

catch the negligible EMF generated by them

- Even though the normal situations prevent them even to move a feather physically but in special situations (we need to research to find the special factors which when the present result in their attaining colossal physical power which can do destruction) the spirits can move big machines even without electricity. This means that spirits under rare special conditions may gain sufficient mechanical power to cause huge destruction.
- Their presence can affect the temperature of surroundings but the effect is very very small and needs special gadgets to record the change in temperature
- They move subtly and their movement can only be felt using a special gadget the causal survival research must base its research on the above observations brought to light by the paranormal investigators. The causal aspects to be researched could be:
- We need to research to find the barrier which prevents spirits to manifest their presence in forceful apparent ways. The barrier between them and live people needs to be researched.
- We need to research why they release feeble energy, feeble EMF, feeble Electromagnetic fields around them, and why the movement is so feeble that it cannot be caught easily by humans.
- To take it forward, Physics has to advance to research how an entity that possesses low-powered energy can amplify to a peak power –how does it do it and what factors make it responsible, and why it is a rare feat.
- Authors mention a medium Pooja who can sense negative energies released by spirits and based on her sense the gadgets are used to confirm the presence of spirits in the environment. Neuroscience has to advance to explain what makes people like Pooja attain this capability. Probably brain scans of People like Pooja while accomplishing this rare feat could be

preserved and compared with patterns of brain circuitry of people who do not possess the ability.

- Why darkness is needed to communicate entities from the other side of the world. All the incidents involving bizarre acts of spirits or communication with them happen only in darkness. We must understand why light is an adverse factor.
- The incidents do propose that memory and knowledge outlive death. We need to evolve a plausible theory to explain this and must attempt to prove it---Energy Survival theoryby Naresh Kumar (2020) is such a theory that needs to be researched to put it on a scientific foundation.

Another interesting approach could be through the use of Hypnotism to take the subjects to previous lives in the hypnotized states and try to understand what do they say about life after death experiences if they happened to have the same.

In fact, hypnotherapist Michael Newton (2013) gives an account of his 29 subjects who were taken to superconscious states and he made them recall memories of earlier life/lives and the intermediary period. His subjects gave a similar account of their transcendence from death to the spirit world and their getting adjusted in the spirit world by following a standard protocol. The experiences narrated by different subjects in the hypnotized states had striking resemblance and makes us believe that their narrations to be real-life journeys into the spirit world.

I wonder whether hypnotism does bring out true facts while subjects are in trance. If it were true then one could, probably, research the causal aspect through hypnotism.

Maybe, there may emerge more ingenious ways to circumvent the impasse over life after death and carry on the causal survival research.

We may even try to put the above-discussed theories of life after death on a scientific platform by researching into aspects that could lead them towards scientific evidence.

Survival theory talks about the continuation of life in form of immortal souls, Lance storm's theory of Radical Survivalism talks about the continuation of Knowledge Form which replaces the soul of survival theory and Energy survival theory talks about Individual self-energy form (ISEF) which again replaces soul. Thus, the soul in some form or the other is at the core of theories on life after death. Soul or the knowledge form or the ISEF could, in fact, be "Consciousness" which is being given different names in various theories and as per theories, soul, Knowledge form and ISEF do not die with death and hence, consciousness outlives death.

Consciousness is researched scientifically but to date, we do not know much about it and it is still a "hard problem" for scientists. If we want to find out, in scientific terms, what happens after we die, we shall have to explore and research consciousness.

One approach to causal survival research could be the pursuit of research on 'Consciousness".

Another causal survival approach could be to pursue my Extended Energy Survival theory. The theory has answers to all the questions which remained unanswered in other contemporary theories on life after death. But still, some questions are left unanswered which prevent Extended Energy Survival become a scientific theory.

If even faintly believed by Physicists, they should research and find the deeper details about the unanswered questions. i.e., what physical properties could a silver cord have? What could be the mechanisms of insulation between ISEFs in their cobweb-type jelly structures on one hand and between SLEFs in their jelly-type structures on another hand? Also, how do the breaches occur which are momentary? Furthermore, the answer is to be found why the information transfer is one way from SLEFs to their unique ISEF and how the insulation sometimes breaches and information flows back through the silver cord to the Live SLEF where he gains access to its previous transformed SLEF life details?

Maybe more work on Quantum Entanglement can lead us to reach scientific evidence for Extended Energy Survival Theory and we have a scientific explanation of death and the afterlife if we could research and find out the mechanism of insulation/ blockage removal and reconnection. Maybe the above could also be a possible way to do causal research about life after death.

We end the discussions about the reality of life after death which will be revealed only through the Causal Survival Research, which is the only path that will uncover the mystery of death, and after life-the researchers must initiate the research the way brain research proceeded.

The last chapter of the book summarizes the discussions held so far to put Parapsychology on the pedestal of rational thinking.

Chapter 7

Parapsychology- brought on pedestal of rational thinking

In previous chapters, we have discussed why Parapsychology could not be accepted by mainstream science and then discussed each constituent of Parapsychology in a rational unbiased way giving equal importance to proponent and opponent views. The book aims to bring the subject of Parapsychology on the pedestal of rational thinking and this chapter would attempt to summarize our discussions so that parapsychology gets the importance it deserves maintaining a rational approach towards our intent.

As per the Parapsychological Association, "***Parapsychology is supported by twin pillars: open-minded scientific study and rigorous doubt. Both are necessary.***"

Throughout the book, we have tried to keep these pillars intact and tried to do justice to the subject so that credibility for treating the subject in a rational manner is maintained.

The skeptic views have been included in the book because these do a valuable service by focusing on educating the public to detect and reject unscrupulous fraudulent people who mislead the masses. The skeptics are scholars who look at the subject critically and posit their valuable comments, unlike the tricksters who rely on magic and frauds.

Giving importance to skeptical views is important as it prepares us to be more thoughtful and be innovative in our dealing with the subject carefully keeping in mind the opponents' views and trying to find solutions to credible questions raised by skeptics, for example- designing experiments in more careful ways to plug all design flaws.

The following views presented by Parapsychological Association are important:

"Unfortunately, some organizations and individual skeptics fail to do their homework and neglect or misapply the scientific methods they want to protect. The result is arguments that fail when tested against readily available facts. We need a clear-minded look at frontier research by observers willing to give it serious attention. A second opinion from someone not involved is valuable. A dispassionate, objective critique can make the difference between a successful experiment from which we learn, and a failed attempt that wastes an opportunity.

The Parapsychological Association invites critical comments and seeks collaborations with interested skeptics. We know from experience how much this can add to our efforts. For example, Marilyn Schlitz and Richard Wiseman conducted an experiment in which they both ran the same remote staring experiment with the same protocol and subject pool (Schlitz, et al., 2006). The outcome indicated a correspondence of results with experimenter expectation in the first experiment and again in a replication, while a third experiment had ambiguous results. The effort advanced our knowledge about the experimenter effect, and showed the value of collaborations involving psi researchers and skeptics."

It is true, indeed, that the views of genuinely concerned skeptics, if studied critically, are a source of learning which not only adds to our knowledge (***experimenter effect*** as in the above paragraph) but also make our research more penetrative with improved designs to make our research more productive. It is good to note that the reputed skeptics have joined to form organizations to promote the skeptic movement against claims of paranormal, the prominent among them was the Committee for Scientific Investigation of Claims of the Paranormal (CSICOP) founded by humanist Philosopher Paul Kunz. For forming CSICOP, he joined hands with science writer Martin Gardener, psychologist Ray Hymen, and magician James Randi. Caroline Watt (2016) mentions that over the years, CSICOP has helped promote skepticism on a wide variety of topics, including investigations into psychics, work examining the psychology of deception and self-deception, and critiques of laboratory-based parapsychological experiments. Much of this work has been reported at CSICOP conferences and published in their bi-monthly magazine, *Skeptical Inquirer.* In 2006, the organization shortened its name to the Committee for Skeptical Inquiry (SCI).

We have discussed in previous chapters the frauds, tricks, magic in staged shows and skeptics' criticism of experimental research in each field of Parapsychology. Even Survival research which has not progressed to the experimental stage, the criticism of Near-Death Experiences (NDEs) (which could take us to causal research to understand death and after-life phenomena) has gone to the extent that the NDEs were called the hallucinatory state of mind. This was opposed by scientists giving scientific proofs which supported the view that NDEs were real and not hallucinatory. This is illustrated in Erica Simon's book; she goes on to write:

"Are the death visions, exalted moods, and reported death experiences by the dying real, or are they hallucinations?

If you are suffering from 'Cerebral Anoxia' your brain is not getting enough oxygen to operate normally. Cerebral Anoxia was often mentioned by doctors and nurses as one of the likeliest explanations for deathbed visions. To see whether this was the real cause, Osis separated all of the dying people who had hand visions into two groups: those who, in the opinion of doctors and nurses, were suffering from cerebral anoxia, and those who weren't. It turned out that anoxia made no difference. The visions of the dying patients with cerebral anoxia were indistinguishable from those of other patients.

Cerebral Anoxia could not, therefore, be the cause of these experiences.

Deathbed visions cannot be explained by the medical condition of the dying person, nor by the state of his mind, nor by religious or cultural background. How, then, can we explain them?

The only remaining possibility is that these are genuine psyche experiences. Being close to death can apparently create an altered state of consciousness which captures the experience and makes it deeply etched in memory and is reported in detail when a person returns back from the threshold of death.

If we can accept these experiences as glimpses into the beyond death- and Osis's research strongly suggests that we have no alternative— then we are ready to venture further into this astounding world. (pp94,99)

Dr. Osis's research and analysis confirm that the NDE phenomena are not due to hallucination experienced by the brain due to lack of oxygen in the brain (*Cerebral Anoxia)* but are real happenings and can be considered as genuine experiences while we transcend from life towards death and beyond if at all there is life after death.

The NDE incidents found in the literature are in agreement that the mood at the time of death is of happiness due to entering a beautiful environment and we are led to believe that death is not traumatic to the person who is dying. It may be a traumatic experience to the near dear ones whom the departing person is leaving behind in our world and they will feel the pain and undergo bereavement but the person meeting death is experiencing joy and happiness when he is transcending from life to death.

Thus, Near Death Experience beats the argument of skeptics who claimed to dismiss these as mere hallucinations, and research of NDEs could probably be an effective way to research into the reality or otherwise of the phenomena of life after death.

The research on other aspects of Parapsychology could advance to their studies in laboratories and the experimental results could be subjected to statistical tests of significance but the after-life research is lagging behind for the obvious reason that the experiencer cannot come back and narrate the incidents, so we have to take an indirect approach to research the phenomenon and NDE is an effective area of effective research.

Coming to laboratory experiments, be it Rhine's card-guessing experiments, Ganzfeld experiments for telepathy or clairvoyance, dice throwing, and random number generating experiments for psychokinesis; the skeptics have risen against them because of the, then, prevalent inability to get experimental results replicated or they pointed flaws in experimental design leading to sensory leakages. In cases where the replications were achieved and also, they could not find design flaws they have argued that statistically significant results were marginally above chance levels and since the phenomena are extraordinary these warrant extraordinary evidence. Moreover, statistical inference only illustrates the presence of assignable causes but what these assignable causes are is a subject matter of further causal research to establish root causes behind the phenomena. The evidence arising out of experimental parapsychological research has credibility but falls short of taking Parapsychology in the fold of Mainstream science. We discussed the impediments in the first chapter so I will not repeat the same here. I, only, wish to reiterate that the impediments for each aspect be it Telepathy, Clairvoyance, Precognition, Psychokinesis, or research on life after death are enormous and researchers have to toil hard to overcome these impediments

As far as tricks/frauds are concerned; these have been perpetrated by people by staging shows to replicate spontaneous parapsychological phenomena to prove that the rare psychic capabilities are possessed by the tricksters. Such people have enjoyed the fame and riches till they are exposed.

Such breed of people has dimmed the credibility of parapsychological phenomena.

The mystery behind the real spontaneous incidents (not the staged shows) is still not resolved. These incidents cannot be frauds as the happening being spontaneous and sporadic does not give any time for planning frauds/tricks. However, some skeptics have accepted these as being real but brushed these aside as mere 'coincidences". But the frequency of occurring of real spontaneous sporadic paranormal incidents is so large that these, certainly, cannot be coincidences. Hence these cannot be taken lightly and we must investigate to find the mystery behind these. These are the only aspects of parapsychology which have not been torn apart by the skeptics as they cannot find any reason to oppose the realness of the spontaneous sporadic paranormal incidents happening across the globe. These incidents, hence, must be probed and we must research to find out the factors which cause these to happen and whether those could be controlled to obey our commands. What I mean to say is that if we become knowledgeable about the factors which when present in the environment or in the mind/ brain of psychic which are the root cause for the manifestation of the paranormal incident, then, we could evaluate whether those factors can be created humanly and if yes, then the incident could be produced at our will.

Only the spontaneous paranormal cases, if researched, can lead us to the causal root of the parapsychological phenomenon.

Irwin HJ (1999) maintains that a primary role for spontaneous cases is to suggest hypotheses for experimental investigation. Spontaneous cases are "real life" experiences and we must find an explanation for them. We may do experimental ESP research to find statistical significance of the ESP experiments but once that is done, we must endeavor to explain how and why these spontaneous parapsychological experiences happen in our day-to-day life. The collection of spontaneous cases at least serves to remind experimental parapsychologists of the ultimate goal for deciphering the why and how of everyday spontaneous cases because these are real-life paranormal phenomena.

In fact, the research on spontaneous cases must have the primary role to suggest hypotheses for experimental investigations. The analysis of spontaneous cases may open wide avenues for causal parapsychological research. Irwin suggests that if spontaneous ESP experiences tend to occur when the percipient is in a mentally relaxed state, the parapsychologists can examine the effect of relaxation on experimental ESP scoring, then if appropriate go on to explore precisely what specific aspects of relaxation are involved in this relationship and the basis of it. Frequently, experimental parapsychologists have given insufficient cognizance to the indications of case materials for process-oriented research.

White (1992) suggests, "Whether or not the phenomena are paranormal, people do have these (spontaneous) experiences and the students of behavior should be interested to ascertain what is distinctive about the content and personal interpretation of these experiences."

I feel that distinctiveness must be researched to move towards causal research of Parapsychological research. One distinctive aspect common to the spontaneous phenomena related to telepathy, clairvoyance, precognition, and psychokinesis is that they all correlate with the working of the mind. Telepathy is mind to mind connection, Clairvoyance is perception through the mind's eye, Precognition is mind perceiving future events and Psychokinesis is mind-influencing physical matter. Mind is the common factor. What do we know about mind and mind's working?

If we have to understand how and why behind the manifestation of bizarre day-to-day ESP events which have a correlation to the working of the mind, we have to first understand the mind.

The mind does the thinking is known to all but can mind see, if yes, how? Can the mind beat the barrier of time and distance, if yes, how? Can the Mind influence physical matter, if yes, how? To top it all, what is the mind? We use the terms Mind and Brain interchangeably. Are the two same? The questions have logically sprung up from discussions on ESP constituent fields but these may not find answers in the parapsychology domain and parapsychological researchers will look expectantly to medical and neuroscience intelligentsia to enlighten them with logical answers. Do they have answers?

I have excluded Life after death from mind discussions of ESP which correlates with Mind. For Life-after-death the pertinent aspect is "Consciousness" which, again, is a Hard Problem to crack by scientists.

Concentrating on ESP for which the pertinent distinctive aspects are Mind and Brain-Have you ever thought about whether the Mind and Brain are distinct entities? As far as my memory goes, we have been using these terms interchangeably and now when I put forward this question, I realize that, yes, these, could, probably, be different.

Dr Ukachoke Chirapat (2018) says the following about the mind: *"The mind is one thing that has always fascinated and puzzled us. From the physical properties of the mind and those of the brain (the alive, processing brain), it can be concluded that the mind always occurs, exists, and functions with the brain and that the brain always occurs, exists, and functions with the mind. Both never occur alone without the other. They are a unity. Each is the intrinsic, equivalent, but different (non-material vs material) aspect of this unity. From the physical properties of the mind and those of the brain's information-*

processing processes, which are non-material processes, it can be concluded that the mind is the composite of the information-processing processes of the brain. Because the mind is a composite of information-processing processes, it is an informational entity – a non-material entity that is composed of information and information processing, and because the information processing processes that form the mind are innumerable in number and involve information that ranges from simple to very advanced, the mind is an informational entity in a highly advanced form."

Truly said, the mind is an invisible informational entity, I often wonder that we do not see many things but they do exist. Bacteria, for example, can be seen by a microscope but is invisible to the naked eye. Till the Microscope was invented we did not see and know about bacteria but it existed. So, it is logical to say that many things may be existing but since we are not able to see them, we feel that these do not exist. However, it is also true that there are things that we do not see but we know that they exist. For example, we are not able to see "Air" but we know it exists because we can feel its existence. The proof of the existence of air is not by its sight but by the sight of what it does. The cool breeze giving us comfort whereas the storms make their presence felt by the devastating results it leaves after manifesting. Heat is another entity that proves existence by its effect. "Mind" can be an informational energy form that exists but is not visible, its existence is proved by its effect in the form of thoughts that comes to us.

Mr. Ajai R Singh and Shakuntala A Singh (2011) clarify the difference between mind and brain as follows: *The structural entity from which all mental operations arise is the brain. The collection of these functional activities of the brain is called the Mind. The brain is the structural correlate of the Mind. The mind is the functional correlate of the Brain. The brain is a structural entity, Mind is not a structural entity*

Summarizing the understanding we can say that the mind is informational energy which is the functional correlate of the brain and the brain is the structural entity where the processing of mental activities happens.

Mind is the common factor in all ESP phenomena. If we have to have clarity about why and how of these phenomena, further research in mind is absolutely necessary; just understanding the definition as above will not be sufficient and since the brain is connected with the mind, the mind research will not be complete without researching the brain.

In discussions on causal research for Telepathy and Clairvoyance, we could explore the brain areas which may be connected to these fields of parapsychology. As discussed, there are areas in the brain that get activated in psychics during these psychic feats whereas in non-psychics the areas remain inactivated. Why and how of this brain aspect needs to be further investigated. The brain is yet to be researched for its 2/3rd part which is still not understood. Further research on the brain will lead us to a better understanding of the mind and eventually the door will open to have clearer knowledge about why and how of all ESP events.

Parapsychology deals in ESP and also in survival research. Mind and brain research will open doors for clarity in ESP phenomena, but for Causal Survival Research the pertinent aspect is "Consciousness", research is needed to understand "Consciousness". The causal research on life after death has not proceeded well because we have still not understood consciousness. Without understanding consciousness, the proponents and opponents are clashing in arguments whether consciousness survives death; proponents believe that consciousness outlives death and continues in some form or the other-be it the soul, knowledge form, or the subtle energy entity ISEF. The contrary view is held by opponents who believe consciousness perishes with death. The clash is meaningless when we do not even understand what consciousness is!!

There are many views on consciousness but a scientific understanding is yet to develop which will give a clue about after-life.

My thoughts on consciousness were developed by adding my logical reasoning to the thoughts of various thinkers. The updated understanding of "consciousness" which is still not complete to become scientific is given in the paper by me, Naresh Kumar (2020). A further way forward to bring scientific understanding to consciousness is also provided in the paper. The consolidated summary is given below:

Logical thinking and consolidation of thoughts by various thinkers, we can say that Consciousness is an invisible non-material informational entity, which cannot be computed, which may or may not be residing in the body and is actually a special kind of re-entrant signaling state; however, the re-entrant signaling state leaves much to be explained viz how the signaling state is achieved, what causes it and how it is constructed?

One thing, though appears true that Consciousness is different from life, it may be different from mind and brain but does have a strong correlation with them. It may or may not reside in the brain but we are not sure till neuroscience advances to find a circuitry in the brain which triggers consciousness or finds the location in the brain where consciousness resides if at all it does reside in the body of living species.

However, it is a fact that the brain, as well as mind, are relevant to consciousness and that the Brain and Mind are interconnected. The Brain is a physical entity and the Mind is a non-physical informational entity and is the processing part of the brain.

The brain is the structural correlate of the mind, and the mind is the functional correlate of the brain. The functions as per the structural changes occurring in the brain activate different parts of the body triggered by Consciousness.

Consciousness, in normal parlance, is awareness—being active, thinking, and performing actions, however, even during aware moments, we can drift to do motor actions unconsciously and during unaware moments life continues with the brain switching to auto mode for performing breathing and pulsating of heart. So it will be erroneous to say that consciousness is only awareness!!

There are divergent views on Consciousness scientists, the most appealing scientific theory is put forward by Roger Penrose and Hameroff, which posits the following views on consciousness –

"Elementary acts of consciousness are non-algorithmic, i.e., non-computable, and they are neurophysiologically realized as gravitation-induced reductions of coherent superposition states in microtubule. The respective quantum states are assumed to be coherent superpositions of tubulin states, ultimately extending over many neurons. Their simultaneous gravitation-induced collapse is interpreted as an individual elementary act of consciousness."

It appears that they hold a view that consciousness does reside in the Brain and manifests in special situations related to quantum reduction theories on the physics side and situations related to *coherent superposition states of microtubule* on the Neuroscience side.

We are not yet certain whether the theory put forth by Penrose and Hameroff is accepted by science because already a lot of criticism has surfaced over that theory and debates continue.

All the above tends to leave us still wonderstruck as to how the consciousness manifests, where does it reside, and whether it is perishable or eternal.

If "Consciousness" does not reside in the brain then it is most probable that there is life after death because then it is probable that consciousness does not perish with death.

On the other hand, if research establishes that "Consciousness has its place within the body of living beings, we remain at crossroads because then both possibilities remain open-there may not be any after-life because consciousness could perish with the body; on the other hand, the possibility is that on death the consciousness could get released from the body in the way soul exits the body and then there is a possibility that after-life is possible

Thus, we see that mere the knowledge of residence of consciousness gives clue about after-life. If we know scientifically what consciousness is then the mystery of life after death will find a clue.

Mind, Brain, and Consciousness if understood will push us in a better understanding of all aspects of Parapsychology. While the researchers in Parapsychology, medicine, psychology, neuroscience, and physics must collaborate to take causal research forward towing the approaches laid down for each component of parapsychology in the foregoing chapters, a deep thrust to our pursuit is possible only through scientific Mind, Brain, Consciousness research.

I shall conclude the book by saying that when we think of the Parapsychology field, we find ourselves in the same condition of primitives who believed that Lightning, Thunderstorm, and Rainbows were paranormal incidences that were spontaneous, sporadic but frequently happening; as are the parapsychological phenomena. Thunder, Lightning, and Rainbows must have frightened the primitive man as Paranormal events which ultimately became casual and normal events when science advanced and gave causal reasons not only for their manifestation but also explained the conditions which made these happen. How true appear the immortal words of St. Augustine, who, once said, "Miracles do not happen in contradiction to nature but only in contradiction to that which is known to us of nature." I am sure miracle will happen only through causal parapsychological research and the knowledge of nature will advance through the combined causal research efforts of Parapsychologists, Neuroscientists, and Physicists, and Medical researchers who will eventually get to reveal to the world the causal reasons not only for the manifestation of parapsychological phenomena but will also reveal the conditions in nature which make them happen. Then the paranormal happening of Parapsychological phenomena will no longer remain paranormal and the bizarre human perception of parapsychological feats will get explained in psychological terms and Parapsychology will, then, become irrelevant and will become a part of Modern Psychology.

References

Chapter 1- Why Parapsychology still not mainstream science

Alcock J E (2003) "give the null hypothesis a chance—a reason to remain doubtful about existence of PSI"—Journal of consciousness studies, 10, No. 6-7 2003, pp 29-50

Blackmore S (1982)-Beyond the body: An investigation of Out-of-the-Body-Experiences, London, Heinemann

Blank, O., Ortigue, S., Landis,T., and Seeck. M (2002)-Stimulating illusory own-body perceptions. Nature, 419, 269-70. Available at https://hpenlaboratory.uchicago.edu/sites/caciopponeurolab.uchicaago.edu/files/uploads/Ortigue_Nature2002.pdf

Broad, C.D(1949) "Violations of Basic limiting Principles" (excerpts) in Readings in Philosophical problems of Parapsychology, A.Flow , ed Ny Prometheus Books

Gelder Tom Van—Phenomenology- The 12 senses *tomvangelder.antrovista.com/sense-of-thought-134m50.html*

Hannah J, University of Tasmania, Australia "Beyond Beliefs: explanation of Anomalous Phenomena"

Hyman Ray (1996)— "Evaluation of a programme on Anomalous mental phenomena" (Journal of scientific exploration, volume 10, No. 1, pp31-58, 1996)

Irwin H (1985) Flight of Mind: A psychological study of Out-of-Body Experience. Metuchen, NJ: Scarecrow Press

Irwin H J (1999) – An introduction to Parapsychology-third edition. Mcfarland & company, Inc. Publishers, Box 611, Jefferson, North Carolina 28640

John Beloff (1980) "Could there be a physical explanation for PSI" (Journal of the Society for Psychical Research, volume 50, No.783, March1980)

Jessica Utts(1999)-"The significance of Statistics in Mind Matter Research"(Journal of Scientific exploration, volume 13, No. 4, pp 615-639, 1996)

Mattuck R.D (1982) "Some possible thermal quantum fluctuation models for Psychokinetic influence on light" (Psychoenergetic , 4 , pp 211-25, 1982)

Michael O' Shea (2005) "The Brain---a very short introduction" published by Oxford Unversity Press, Inc. New York, 2005

Philosophy & Paranormal—Transcript of Radio Programme Broadcast by 2SER FM in conjunction with U.N.E

Rhine J B (1937) New frontiers of mind (NY: Farrar & Rinchart, 1937)

Schmeidler G. R., & Mcconnell R. A. (1958). ESP and Personality Patterns. New Haven: Yale University Press.

Soal S.G & Bateman, F (1954) Modern experiments in telepathy (New Heaven, CT: Yale University Press)

Targ & Puthoff H E (1974) "Information transfer under conditions of sensory shielding" (Nature , 252,p 602 , 1974)

Walker (1984) "Acknowledging and dealing with fear of PSI phenomenon" (journal of Parapsychology, 48,pp272-332, 1984)

Wiseman R (2011) "Paranormality—why we see what isn't there" published in july2011 by Mcmillan.

Wiseman R. and Morris R.L. (1995)- Guidelines for testing Psychic Claimants. Hatfield, University of Hertfordshire Press.

Chapter2- Telepathy-on rational pedestal

ANNEMANN. (1938, August). Was Prof. J. B. Rhine hoodwinked? *Jinx*, No. 47, 329, 333.

COOVER, J. E. (1917). *Experiments in Psychical Research at Leland Stanford Junior University*. Stanford, CA: Stanford University.

Dewey Catlin (2015). Mark Zuckerberg says the future of communication is telepathy. Here's how that would actually work. *washingtonpost.com/news/the-intersect/wp/2015/07/01/mark-zuckerberg-says-the-future-of-communication-is-telepathy-heres-how-that-would-actually-work/*

DINGWALL, E. J. (1956). The simulation of telepathy. In G. E. W. Wolstenholme & E. C. P. Millar (Eds.), *Ciba Foundation Symposium on Extrasensory Perception* (pp. 141–147). Boston: Little, Brown.

Elkin, A P (1937). Notes on psychic life of the Australian Aborigines, Mankind, 2(3), 49-56

Elkin A P (1945/77). Aboriginal men of high degree (2nd ed). St. Lucia: University of Queensland Press.

ESTABROOKS, G. H. (1947). *Spiritism*. New York: Dutton.

GAULD, A. (1965a). Letter to the editor. *Journal of the Society for Psychical Research*, 43, 220–224.

GAULD, A. (1965b). Mr[.] Hall and the S.P.R. *Journal of the Society for Psychical Research*, 43, 53–62.

G[URNEY], E. (1888). Note relating to some of the published experiments in thought-transference. *Proceedings of the Society for Psychical Research*, 5, 269–270.

GURNEY, E., MYERS, F. W. H., PODMORE, F., & BARRETT, W. F. (1883). Third report on thought-transference. *Proceedings of the Society for Psychical Research*, 1, 161–215.

HALL, T. H. (1964). *The Strange Case of Edmund Gurney*. London: Gerald Duckworth.

HANSEL, C. E. M. (1959, April 30). Experiments on telepathy. *New Scientist*, 5, 983–984.

Hansen George P (1990). Deception by subjects in psi research. The Journal of the American Society for Psychical Research. Vol. 84, No.1. January 1990 pp25-80 *tricksterbook.com/Articlesonline/DeceptionFraudTrickeryParapsychology,html*

Hehe Joshua, 2019. Telepathy—Mind to mind communication. medium.com/@joshuashawnmichaelhehe/telepathy-279db521f69c

Hutson Matthews (2018), "Mind-reading algorithm can decode the pictures in your head". https://www.sciencemag.org/news/2018/01/mind-reading-algorithm-can-decode-pictures-your-headr3f_986=https:/www.google.com/

Irwin H J (1999). An introduction to Parapsychology -3rd edition. McFarland & Company, Inc. Publishers, Jefferson, North Carolina, and London

Kumar Naresh (2020)- What if ESP(The sixth sense is real). International Journal of Social Impact ISSN: 2455-670X Volume 5, Issue 3, DIP: 18.02.007/20200503 DOI: 10.25215/2455/0503007 www.ijsi.in |July - September 2020

Kumar Naresh (2021)—Parapsychology -Trending towards Causal Research. Redshine Publications Pvt. Ltd., 88, Patel Street, Navamuvada, Lunawada, India-389230 in association with Red'Mac International Press & Media. Inc. India/ Sweden/ Canada

Lewis Ralph (2019); What actually is a thought? How is information physical; Psychology Today 2019. Wwwpsychologytoday.com/us/blog/finding purpose/2019/02/what-actually-is a-thought-how-is- information-physical/

MORRIS, R. L. (1978). A survey of methods and issues in ESP research. In S. Krippner (Ed.), *Advances in Parapsychological Research 2: Extrasensory Perception* (pp. 7–58). New York: Plenum.

MUNDLE, C. W. K. (1959). Review of The Mind Readers by S. G. Soal and H. T. Bowden. *Journal of the Society for Psychical Research*, 40, 84–96.

NICOL, B. H. (1960). The Jones boys: A case for telepathy not proven. *Journal of the American Society for Psychical Research*, 54, 118–135.

NICOL, J. F. (1960). Keeping up with the Joneses. *Tomorrow*, 8(1), 58–66.

Parapsychological Association (feb 11, 2011)- Why is Parapsychology so controversial *parapsychology.org/articles/36/56/why_is_parapsychology_so.aspx*

Persinger Michael A & Saroka Kevin S (2012). Protracted Parahippocampal activity associated with Sean Harribance ncbi.nlm.gov/pmc/articles/PMC34101541/

Taylor, John, A NEW THEORY FOR ESP, Journal 62, 1998, pp 289-310.

Radin Dean (2006), "Entangled Minds, extrasensory experiences in a quantum reality, Paraview,191 seventh avenue, New York, NY10011

Ramachandran V S (2012)—The Tell-Tale Brain. Random House Publishers India Private limited, Windsor IT Park, 7th floor, Tower B, a-1 sector-125, Noida-201301, UP.

RHINE, J. B., & PRATT, J. G. (1962). *Parapsychology: Frontier Science of the Mind*. Springfield, IL: Charles C Thomas. (Original work published 1957)

SCOTT, C., & GOLDNEY, K. M. (1960). The Jones boys and the ultra-sonic whistle. *Journal of the Society for Psychical Research*, 40, 249–260.

SOAL, S. G., & BOWDEN, H. T. (1960). *The Mind Readers*. Garden City, NY: Doubleday.

SOAL, S. G. (1959). Letter to the editor. *Journal of the Society for Psychical Research*, 40, 200–203.

SOAL, S. G. (1960). The Jones boys; the case against cheating. *Journal of the Society for Psychical Research*, 40, 291–299.

TARG, R., & PUTHOFF, H. (1974, November 7). Geller: Experimenters reply. *New Scientist*, 64, 443.

Tesla Nikola (1933) "tremendous New power soon to be released" Kansas City Journal-post Sept 10, 1933

THOULESS, R. H. (1961). Were the Jones boys signalling by Morse code? *Journal of the American Society for Psychical Research*, 55, 24–28.

Venkatasubramanian Ganesan, Jayakumar Peruvumba, Nagendra Hongasandra, Nagaraja Dindagur, Deeptha R, Gangadhar Bangalore (2008). Investigating paranormal phenomena: Functional brain imaging of Telepathy. International Journal of Yoga (2008-01-01), Vol no.1,No.2, pp66-71

Watt Caroline (2016)- Parapsychology-Beginners Guide. Published in North America, Great Britain and Australia by Oneworld Publications, 201605\96

Chapter 3—Clairvoyance / Remote viewing- on rational pedestal

Alcock, J. (2003). Give the null hypothesis a chance: Reasons to remain doubtful about the existence of Psi. *Journal of Consciousness Studies*, *10*, 29–50.

Bem, D. J., & Honorton, C. (1994). Does Psi exist? Replicable evidence for an anomalous process ofinformation transfer. *Psychological Bulletin*, *115*, 4–18.

Carroll Todd (1994)-The Skeptic's Dictionary-psychic *skepdic.com /psychic.html*

Edge, H. L., Morris, R. L., Palmer, J., & Rush, J. H. (1986). *Foundations of parapsychology*. London:Routledge & Kegan Paul.

ESP Researchers forum (2008ESP). ESP Researchers---Researchers Encyclopedia of the Unusual and Unexplained:: Mysteries of the Mind

Hyman, R. (1994). Anomaly or artifact? Comments on Bem and Honorton. *Psychological Bulletin*, *115*, 19–24.

Irwin H J (1999). An introduction to Parapsychology -3rd edition. McFarland & Company, Inc. Publishers, Jefferson, North Carolina, and London

Dr. Murphy Joseph, (2014). Psychic Perception—The magic of Extrasensory Power. Manjul Publishing House, 7/32, Ansari Road, DaryaGanj, New Delhi 110002.

Parapsychological Association (2011)- Remote viewing. *parapsych.org/articles/36/63/4_remote_viewing.aspx*

Playfair Lyon Guy (2014)- Richard Wiseman's Remote Viewing "Breakthrough". The association for skeptical investigation. *https://www.skepticalaboutskeptics.org/investigating-skeptics/whos-who-of-media-skeptics/richard-wiseman/richard-wisemans-remote-viewing-breakthrough/*

Sonali Bhatt Marwaha and Prof Edwin C May (2019;)Informational Psi –collapsing the problem space of psi phenomena; Zeitscrift fur Anomalistik, vol 19(2019) pp 12-51

Utts, J. (1991). Replication and meta-analysis in parapsychology. *Statistical Science*, *6*(4), 363–403.

Wiseman Richard, Schlitz, Watt Caroline (2006)- Of two minds: Sceptic proponent collaboration within parapsychology. British Journal of Psychology (2006) 97,313-322 *richardwiseman.com/resources/twominds.pdf*

Chapter 4-Precognition—on rational pedestal

Bancel Peter and Mario Varvoglis (2015)—A paper on Micro-psychokinesis *researchgate.net/ publication/ 273889027_Micro-psychokinesis*

Boyle Alan (2011). Psychic proof? Skeptics strike back, article by Science Editor, NBC News -jan7, 2011 *https://www.nbcnews.com/science/cosmic-log/psychic-proof-skeptics-strike-back-flna6c10403534*

Carroll Robert Todd (1994)—Clairvoyance or second sight—the skeptics dictionary. *skepdic.com/clairvoy.html*

Cox, W. E. (1956) Precognition: An analysis, II. *Journal of the American Society for Psychical Research, 50*, 99-109.

Fields R Douglous (2008) – "Mind control by cell phones" paper in Scientific American May 7, 2008 link scientificamerican.com/article/mind-control-by-cell/

Lehrer Jonah – Feeling the Future: Is Precognition possible? *wired.com/2010/11/feeling-the-future-is-precognition-possible/*

Marwaha Sonali Bhatt and Prof Edwin C May (2015;)Rethinking Extrasensory Perception: Towards a Multiphasic Model of Precognition; SAGE Open January-March 2015: 1–17

May, E. C., & Spottiswoode, S. J. P. (2014). Shannon entropy: A possible intrinsic target property. In E. C. May & S. B. Marwaha (Eds.), *Anomalous cognition: Remote viewing research and theory* (pp. 299-313). Jefferson, NC: McFarland. (Original work published 1994)

May, E. C., Lantz, N. D., & Piantineda, T. (2014). Feedback considerations in anomalous cognition experiments. In E. C. May & S. B. Marwaha (Eds.), *Anomalous cognition: Remote viewing research and theory* (pp. 104-116). Jefferson, NC: McFarland. (Original work published 1996)

Radin Dean (2006)—Book Entangled Minds. Pocket Books, a division of Simon & Schuster. Inc. 1230 Avenue of the Americas, New York, NY 10020. ISBN-13:978-1-4165-1677- 4(pp 250-260)

Shannon, C. E., & Weaver, W. (1949). *The mathematical theory of communication*. Urbana: University of Illinois Press.

Verlinde, E. (2011). On the origin of gravity and the laws of Newton. *Journal of High Energy Physics, 4*, 1-27.

Schwarzkopf D. S. (2014). We should have seen this coming. Front. Hum. Neurosci. 8:332 10.3389/fnhum.2014.00332 [PMC free article] [PubMed] [CrossRef] [Google Scholar]

Stevenson, I. (1960). A review and analysis of paranormal experiences connected with the sinking of the Titanic. Journal of American Society for Psychical Research, 54, 153–171

Watt Caroline (2017) – Precognition: From Life to Lab *kostlerunit.wordpress.com/2017/06/06/precognition-from-life-to-lab/*

Watt C., L. Vuillaume & R. Wiseman (2015)- Dream Precognition and Sensory Incorportation: A Controlled Sleep Laboratory Study— Journal of Consciousness https://philpapers.org/rec/WATDPA

Watt C, Marilyn Schlitz, Richard Wiseman, and Dean Radin, 2006 Of two minds: Sceptic–proponent collaboration within parapsychology British Journal of Psychology (2006), 97, 313–322 The British Psychological Society

Wiseman R (2011) "Paranormality—why we see what isn't there" published in july 2011 by Mcmillan.

Chapter 5-Psychokinesis-On rational pedestal

Bosch Holger, Fiona Steinkamp, and Emil Boller (2006). Examining psychokinesis: The interaction of human intention with random number generators- A meta-analysis. Psychological Bulletin 132(4):497-523, August 2006 DOI:10.1037/0033-2909.132.4.497

Jessica Utts(1999)-"The significance of Statistics in Mind Matter Research"(Journal of Scientific exploration, volume 13, No. 4, pp 615-639, 1996)

Maier Markus A. , Dechamps Moritz C. and Pflitsch Markus (2018) (Department of Psychology, Ludwig-Maximilians-Universität München, Munich, Germany)--- Intentional Observer Effects on

Quantum Randomness: A Bayesian Analysis Reveals Evidence Against Micro-Psychokinesis. Published in Front. Psychol., 21 March 2018 | https://doi.org/10.3389/fpsyg.2018.00379

Sukma Raga (2009)-History of Psychokinesis. May 4, 2020, *ghaibiyah.blogspot.com/2009/05/history-of- psychokinesis.html*

Strange Sounds (2016)- The psychic powers of Nina Kulagina are just too crazy. Published on February 24,2016. *strangesounds.org/2016/02/telekinesis-psychic-nina-kulagina-video.html*

Varvoglis Mario, (2020). Psychokinesis (PK) - The Parapsychological Association. published by View Rick E Berger, PhD's profile Rick E Berger, PhD on Friday, February 14, 2020.

Watt Caroline (2016)- Parapsychology-Beginners Guide. Published in North America, Great Britain and Australia by One world Publications, 201605\96

Chapter 6- Life After Death- Does it exist

Berger, A. S. (1995). The aristocracy of the dead: New findings in post-mortem survival. Je›erson, NC: McFarland.

Botkin, A. I., with Hogan, R. C. (2005). Induced after-death communication: A new therapy for healing grief and trauma. Charlottesville, VA: Hampton Roads.

Brennan Siofra. (2016)-People who had near-death experience explain what dying REALLY feels like.

Braude, S. E. (2003). Immortal remains: The evidence for life after death. NY: Rowman & Littlefield.

Carroll Sean M (2011) Physics and the Immortality of the Soul, Scientific American May 23, 2011. https://blogs.scientific*amaerican.com/guest-blog-/physics-and-the-immortality-of-the-soul/*

Chopra Deepak (2006)—Life After Death-The Book of answers. Published by Harmony Books, USA *dailymail.co.uk/femail/article-3437192/People-believe-ve-experienced-death-explain-REALLY-feels-like.html*

Devers, E. (1994). Experiencing the deceased. Florida Nursing Review, 1 (3), 7–13.

Drewry, M. D. L. 2002. Purported after-death communication and its role in the recovery of bereaved individuals: A phenomenological study. Unpublished doctoral dissertation, San Diego, CA: California Institute for Human Science.

Ennamorato Judith (2006) Astrals, Auras & Apparitions: A Compendium of the Paranormal; Trafford Publishing, 6E- 2333, Government St., Victoria,BC V8T 4P4 CANADA

Flew, A. (1953). A New Approach to Psychical Research. London: Watts.

Freud, S. (1962). Thoughts for the times on war and death: Our attitude towards death. In J. Strachey (Eand trans.), The standard edition of the complete psychological works of Sigmund Freud (Vol. 14, pp. 289–300). London: Hogarth Press. (Original work published 1915).

Hansen 2001. Prominent "psychics". G. P. Hansen, *The trickster and the paranormal* (Chapter 10). Philadelphia,PA: Xlibris Corporation.

Hill W E--- Painting entitled "My wife and mother-in-law Indian Holy Book "Bhagwad Gita."

James, W. (2002). Varieties of religious experience. London: Routledge; Taylor & Frances Group. (Original work published 1902).

Krippner, S. (2000). Spotted Fawn's farewell. In L. Lawson, Visitations from the afterlife: True stories of love and healing (pp. 87–88). San Francisco: HarperSanFrancisco.

Kumar Naresh (2020)- Life After Death: Contemporary Theories and Beyond. International Journal of Social Impact ISSN: 2455-670X Volume 5, Issue 2, DIP: 18.02.001/20200502 DOI: 10.25215/2455/0502001 www.ijsi.in |April-June, 2020

Kumar Naresh (2021)- book- What happens when and after we die. Red'Shine Publications Pvt Ltd. 88, Patel Street, Navamuvada, Lunawada, India, 389230.

LaGrand, L. (1999). Messages and miracles: Extraordinary experiences of the bereaved. St. Paul, MN: Llewellyn.

M Shange of Clarkson University—fungal pore and Haunting experiences Michael Persinger---electromagnetic radiations impact on brain

Milgram (1974) Obedience to authority, New York, NY: Harper

Mohanty Sarabjeet, D'Silva Neil (2020)- The spirits talk to me (True accounts of Paranormal Investigations). Published by Hachette Book Publishing India Pvt. Ltd., 4th & 5th Floors, Corporate Centre, Plot no. 94, Sector 44, Gurugram 122003, India

Dr. Murphy Joseph, (2014). Psychic Perception—The magic of Extrasensory Power. Manjul Publishing House, 7/32, Ansari Road, Darya Ganj, New Delhi 110002.

Myers F (1903) Human personality and its Survival of bodily death. London, Longmans Green

Moreman C. M. (2006). Mystical experience and the afterlife. In L. Storm & M. A. Thalbourne (Eds.), The survival of human consciousness: Essays on the possibility of life after death (Chapter 2). Jefferson, NC: McFarland.

Newton Michael (2013, 2021)-Journey of Douls—case studies of Life between Lives. Published by Jaico Publishing House A-2 Jash Chambers, 7-A Sir Phirozshah Mehta Road, Fort, Mumbai-400001 ISBN 978-81-8495-105-9 First Jaico impression: 2013 ; 12th Jaico impression:2021

Parker, J. S. (2004). After death communication experiences and adaptive grief outcomes. Unpub- lished doctoral dissertation. San Francisco: Saybrook Graduate School and Research Center.

The philosophy Book (2011) Published in Great Britain in 2011 by Dorling Kindersley Limited, 80 Strand, London, WC2R 0RL- A Penguin Random House Company

Ramachandran V.S. (2010)—The Tell-Tale Brain, Random House Publishers limited, Windsor IT Park, 7th Floor, Tower B, A-1, Sector-125, Noida-201301 U.P. ISBN 978 81 8400 207 2

Rooper Allan (2014) – Excerpt- "How doctors determine the moment of death" from the book "Reaching down the rabbit hole". *Scientificamerican.com/article/how-doctors-determine-the-moment-of-death-excerpt/*

Ross, L. & Nisbett, R. (1991). The person and the situation. New York, NY: McGraw-Hill.

Ryan Mark B—The resurrection of Frederic Myers. (*atpweb.org/jtparchive/trps-42-10-02-149.pdf*)

Simon Erica (2006) Life After Death, Published by Sahni Publications, Delhi 2006

Sudduth Michael (2009), Journal of scientific Explorations, Vol23, no.2, pp167-193, 2009.

Susana Martinez Conde 2018. Brain's region for Pareidola.

Taylor Steve (2018)- Transformation through Dying—The aftermath of near-death experiences. *psychologytoday.com/us/blog/out-the-darkness/201811/transformation-through -dying*

Watt Caroline (2016)- Parapsychology-Beginners Guide. Published in North America, Great Britain and Australia by One world Publications, 201605\96

Villines Zawn (2020)- How long does it take to get pregnant after sex-In Medical News today. *medicalnewstoday.com/articles/how-long-does-it-take-to-get-pregnant*

Zamit Victor—Excerpts from his book, " A Lawyer presents the evidence for after life". The excerpt appeared as an article –*near-death.com/parapsychology/psychics/Frederic-myers.html*

Zimbardo, P. (1969). The human choice: Individuation, reason and order versus deindividuation, impulse and chaos. In W. J. Arnold & D. Levine (Eds.), Nebraska symposium on motivation (Vol. 17). Lincoln, NE: University of Nebraska Press.

Chapter 7 Parapsychology-on rational pedestal

Ajai R. Singh*, Shakuntala A. Singh (2011), Brain, Mind and Consciousness—An integrated interdisciplinary perspective. MSM print, ISSN 0973-1229 E ISSN 1998-4014—Mens Sena monographs (2011) vol. 9, No. 1, Jan-dec 2011 ISBN 978-81-89753-19-1

Article that Appeared in THE FREE PRESS JOURNAL—Mumbai, Thursday January 30,2014--Unique brain area behind better decision –making.

Eagleman David, (2011) – book Incognito-The secret lives of the brain. Published by Canongate Books Ltd., 14 high street, Edinburg EHi iTE ISBN978 I 84767 9383

Irwin H J (1999). An introduction to Parapsychology -3rd edition. McFarland & Company, Inc. Publishers, Jefferson, North Carolina, and London

Kumar Naresh (2020). Consciousness-some conscious thoughts. The International Journal of Indian Psychology ISSN 2348-5396 (Online) | ISSN: 2349-3429 (Print) Volume 8, Issue 4, Oct- Dec, 2020. DIP: 18.01.104/20200804 DOI: 10.25215/0804.104

Kumar Naresh (2020)—Parapsychology-Towards Causal Research. International Journal of Social Impact ISSN: 2455-670X Volume 5, Issue 2, DIP: 18.02.010/20200502 DOI: 10.25215/2455/0502010 www.ijsi.in |April-June, 2020

Smith (2017), Nikola Tesla's wildest project – the Thought projector--- *www.disclose.tv.nikola-teslas-wildest-project-the-thought-projector-314535*

Dr Ukachoke Chirapat (2018)—Book- The basic Theory of Mind. Original edition May 12, 2018 and final edition in Feb 20, 2020 from Generate Press.

White R A (1992) Review of approaches to the study of spontaneous psi experiences. *Journal of scientific Exploration., 6, 93-126*